TEA LEAVES

Journeys to the Tea Lands

RON VERZUH

RON VERZUH

The cover photograph features an aging tea worker on one of the Darjeeling tea estates.

RON VERZUH

OTHER BOOKS BY RON VERZUH

Underground Times
Canada's Flower-Child Revolutionaries

Radical Rag
Canada's Pioneer Labour Press

TO LEOLA

RON VERZUH

"TEA IS DRUNK TO FORGET THE DIN OF THE WORLD."
T'ien Yiheng
Essay on Boiling Spring Water
Circa 1570

Billy tea time with the platypuses, echidnas and wombats at the bottom of the world in Tasmania.

"MAKE TEA NOT WAR!"
Car bumper sticker
Circa 2011

A tea merchant in the Chowk Bazaar in Darjeeling, India, blows
on her tea to bring out its full aroma.

"THERE ARE FEW HOURS IN LIFE MORE AGREEABLE THAN THE HOUR DEDICATED TO THE CEREMONY KNOWN AS AFTERNOON TEA."

Henry James
The Portrait of a Lady
Published in 1881

CONTENTS

Serving tea at a palace in Jaipur,
Rajasthan, India.

ACKNOWLEDGMENTS

In my more than thirty years of tea travelling I have been assisted by dozens of tour guides, tea experts, high tea and low tea specialists, taxi drivers, tea ladies, tea men, friends, relatives and total strangers. All were willing to tolerate my tea indulgences and excuse both my tea-related ignorance and occasional excesses. A hearty, tea-warming, scone-munching thank you to all of them. A special thank you to Leola, my love, who is always encouraging and whose faith in me never waivers…even as another 'tea leave' threatens to disrupt our lives. If there is a tea heaven may we all meet there in tea-sipping bliss.

"WE HAD A KETTLE; WE LET IT LEAK:
OUR NOT REPAIRING MADE IT WORSE.
WE HAVEN'T HAD ANY TEA FOR A WEEK…
THE BOTTOM IS OUT OF THE UNIVERSE."

Rudyard Kipling

1 INTRODUCTION

"Tea leaves can be "as wrinkled as the leather on the boots of Tartar riders; as frizzy as the hair on a bull's belly; or as smooth as the mist which rises from a mountain gorge; which shimmer like the spray from the sea and are as soft as the damp earth."

– *Cha Jing, The Holy Book of Tea* or *The Classic of Tea* written by Lu Yu in 780 A.D.

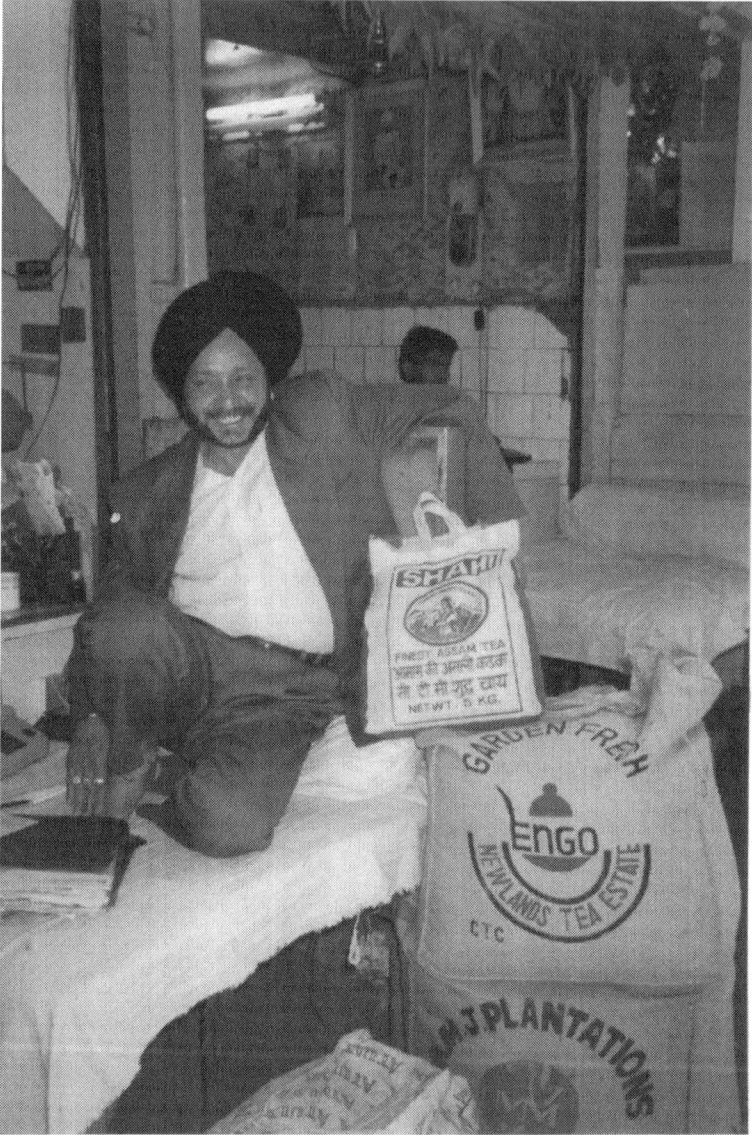

A tea merchant in New Delhi shows off his product.

A Traveller's Passion for Tea
From Victoria to Shanghai to Darjeeling and Down Under

The tea lady woke me with a rap on the door of my clean but tiny room at Dolphin Square, Pimlico, in London. Tea was the last thing on my mind at 7:30 a.m. But this was London, England, where morning tea is a tradition that dates back even before Thomas Twining set up his little tea shop in the Strand in 1706.

"Here's your cuppa, Gov!" said my tea lady as she placed a tray of piping hot PG Tips with milk and biscuits (read cookies) at my bedside. "Hope you like it." It was part of the $65 cost of my room, a steal by London standards in those days even though I had to share a bathroom.

As I sipped the steaming brew I began plotting a day trip to Norwich about two hours to the northeast by train. Why? Well, in a way that was the reason for beginning my tea travels in the first place. I was going to Norwich to visit the largest collection of British ceramic teapots in the world.

That wasn't the only reason, I admit, but the thought of being surrounded by 2,600 of these delightful receptacles of a liquid that had changed the course of so much history was a major drawing card.

My train left from Victoria Station, where the famed Orient Express was awaiting its cargo of rich and famous travellers a few platforms down. Later that day, they would have their tea in the finest of china and silver while I took mine in paper with a plastic stir stick as we sped through the well-farmed countryside that inspired Constable, Turner and Gainsborough.

Norwich sits at the northern tip of East Anglia, which includes the university town of Cambridge, several delightful fishing villages, and some of the earliest Roman encampments in Britain. This is also windmill country and the home of the Norfolk Broads, a holiday lake district.

It's an ancient city, almost a thousand years old, with plenty of medieval buildings, streets and cultural traditions to prove it. But my

19

interest on that day was teapots. These were housed in Norwich's Norman castle, a short bus ride from the train station and an even shorter hike up several winding layers of stone stairs.

Perched above the "fine old city," as the writer George Borrow described Norwich over 100 years ago, the castle had been converted to a museum that included the Twining Teapot Gallery. The museum clerk directed me straight to where the holy grail of tea artefacts might be hiding and within moments I was standing before two long banks of glass display cases running from floor to ceiling. Here was the tea lover's Treasure of the Sierra Madre, the tea aficionado's Garden of Earthly Delights. The Da Vinci Code of tea was to found here, if anywhere, and it had been broken.

The pots were stacked in orderly rows, dated, and including a brief explanation of who the original owner was and any unusual characteristics that should be observed. There were round, oval and hand-sculptured pots of all colours, dating from the early eighteenth century to the present. Most of the early pots borrowed designs and painted images from the Chinese porcelain teapots that came tucked away in wooden tea chests. These were once rushed across the world by speedy tea clipper to find their place in the British upper class's delicately carved tea caddies so elegantly displayed at afternoon social sippings.

The pots came in all sizes, but they were usually small because tea was so expensive. In those days, a pound of tea could cost a skilled worker a week's wages, so only the wealthy could indulge in this most British of British pastimes. That lasted until the late 1700s when the price of ale soared and tea merchants successfully lobbied to have tea taxes lowered making it affordable to all. Cheaper tea after 1784 brought larger teapots once reserved for the serving of punch.

There were pots made of stoneware, creamware, caneware, pearlware and earthenware. They were made by Wedgewood, Minton and Spode. They came shaped as monkeys, fish, camels, cauliflowers and castles. One incredible pot was shaped from the entwined bodies of a serpent and a rooster. The spout was formed from the bird's beak biting into the snake's neck; the handle was the reptile's writhing tail.

Some had poems or prayers or political messages inscribed on them, others were glazed to look like marble, and some included woodcuts and other images set under gold-tinted glazes. The rose, the most common of tea lid ornaments was everywhere in evidence, but it was rivalled by the occasional lion, fish or swan.

My thirst for teapots adequately quenched, I stopped for tea and scones at the museum tearoom. Next door, a gift shop displayed several of the more modern novelty teapots often seen in gift shops everywhere. On the shop bookshelf was a massive study of teapots by Norwich museum decorative arts curator Robin Emmerson called *British Teapots and Tea Drinking*. In it, he documents the history of tea and the teapot, including its place in the key moments of history.

"Tea-drinking held an important place in Georgian social life," wrote Emmerson. "It embodied people's desire to live in a stylish, refined...way. The teapot's importance as a fashionable item of consumer goods explains why such inventiveness was lavished on its design."

I glanced at the book just until I had finished my tea, disappointingly brewed with a bag instead of loose leaves, and then took a quick tour of Norwich's fine old Norman cathedral, with its 15th-century spire. Soon I was on a train back to London.

***

My tea lady was right on time the next morning with the usual offering. But I declined. I had spied an evergreen-coloured shed near the Pimlico tube station. I had heard about the green shacks, but never noticed them before. They looked much like a construction workers' portable.

I strolled up to my discovery at about 10 a.m. and the owner greeted me from her steamy window, old tea mugs, some chipped around the edges, dangling from its perimeter.

"Allo, then," she said in a fine Cockney accent. "What you snoopin' around 'ere for?" I explained that I had heard about London's tea sheds. A lady from the British Tea Council once told me that they served the most delicious cup of tea in England. "It's just for cabbies, you know," she said. "But I reckon you can come on in for a cup. Just one, mind."

And so began my passion for tearooms and my tea-slaked wanderlust. It was to be the first of many 'tea leaves' I would take over the next 20 years. Since then, I have taken tea with orangutans in Singapore, with crocodiles on the Great Barrier Reef, with Tibetans in Darjeeling, with the ghost of Agatha Christie in Harrogate, and among the bones of dinosaurs in the Badlands of Alberta.

I have tasted Billy tea, freshly picked estate tea, pure tea, blended tea, expensive tea and bad tea the world over. I have sat in some of the finest tearooms and teahouses in existence. Family, friends and casual acquaintances have suffered through my long babblings about the virtues of cream tea versus high tea, Oolong versus Keemun, my dislike for the taste of bergamot oil in Earl Grey, and the wickedness of using bag tea instead of loose.

***

In my tea travels I have learned that one can divide the world into two kinds of country, two kinds of people, and two kinds of culture: tea drinkers and coffee drinkers. At least that's one way to look at it.

On a tea leave to India, for example, I sat amidst lepers to sip a delicious glass of chai prepared on a street corner by a chaiwallah in Jaipur. I drank the champagne of teas high in the Himalayan foothills at Darjeeling. In China, I saw life at sidewalk level by joining the tea drinkers of Beijing as they smoked and waited patiently for their Spring Bud Jasmine to brew. I ate quail's eggs at the Yu Garden Teahouse in Shanghai where Queen Elizabeth once did the same.

In England, indubitably the world's primo tea country, I fattened on great dollops of Cornish clotted cream tea while reading the West Country's queen of storytelling, Daphne Du Maurier country. I indulged in a "Fat Rascal" at Betty's of Yorkshire, the undisputed queen of British tearooms. I have even paid substantial sums of money to be insulted by the waiters in the Palm Court tearoom at the Ritz in London.

I have indulged my habit at Raffles's Tiffin Room in Singapore where Rudyard Kipling ate fine curries with his tiffin (afternoon tea), then nursed a Singapore Sling at the luxurious hotel's Writer's Bar where Joseph Conrad no doubt played billiards.

My tea leaves have taken me to the tearooms of Thailand where lemon grass tea is the constant favourite, to Hong Kong for tea with dim sum and to Paris for a cup of Marco Polo at Mariage Frères. I have enjoyed an egg-timer-perfect, four-minute (and those are not New York minutes) tea served in the basement of the Guggenheim Art Gallery in New York after a walk along the Great White Way with Walt Whitman under my arm.

I have sipped the golden liquid with kings, queens, princes, princesses, presidents and prime ministers. I have been served the 4,000-year-old elixir before chieftains on fine woven grass mats, diplomats in the poshest of embassies, and with dictators turned peacemakers.

These are the stories of those tea leaves. I hope that they will be as delightfully refreshing as a fine cup of Darjeeling served while you gaze upon the world's treasures and wonders. I further hope that you will share the thrill of finding a tiny space where you can invoke your fantasies and your passions, as I have done, and completely forget the real world for just a few moments.

Before you begin your voyage, a final warning to fellow tea travellers: this is a travel book not a travel guide. Where prices are indicated, they are usually in the dollar equivalent of that year. As well, some of the tearooms you will read about here may no longer exist. Finally, I freely express many opinions about many things in *Tea Leaves* and wish to extend my advance apologies to those readers who may not always share those opinions.

Bon voyage and happy tea drinking. I will see you at the end of your tea leaves.

Ron Verzuh
Eugene, Oregon
January 2012

A chaiwallah prepares tea in Jaipur, Rajasthan.

2 ASIA

"The first cup caresses my dry lips and throat. The second shatters the walls of my lonely sadness. The third searches the dry rivulets of my soul to find the stories of five thousand scrolls. With the fourth the pain of past injustice vanishes through my pores. The fifth purifies my flesh and bones. With the sixth I am in touch with the immortals. The seventh gives such pleasure I can hardly bear."

– From a poem written by Lu Tong during the Tang Dynasty period (619-907 A.D.).

Asia is where the giants of tea reside. It is in China that the myths and majesty of tea history are found. In Himalayan India the great teas grow in the valleys created by the highest mountains on earth. So it is here that our tea journeys begin, here where the magic of tea can consume tea travelers and infect us for a lifetime.

Tea at the Top of the World (Part I)
A Tibetan tea tour of Darjeeling

On the way up to the fabled 'hill station' of Darjeeling, 7,000 feet above sea level in West Bengal, India, I shuddered as we passed hand-lettered signs screaming "We want Gorkha Land." Wouldn't a separatist guerrilla movement here in the foothills of the Himalayas fancy taking me hostage? I flattered myself. And wouldn't they be disappointed to learn that I was just another traveller on a pilgrimage to the ancestral home of the "Champagne of Teas"?

The ride itself had been harrowing enough. I had teamed up with a writer from Birmingham, Alabama, who was on freelance assignment with *Ms.*, the American feminist magazine. She had insisted on taking a jeep up the roughly paved one-track road from Siliguri, a dozen kilometers from Bagdogra airport. It was cheap at forty rupees each (less than $2), but no way to travel for a lady, even a feminist one.

Still, it had to be better than what Nina Mazuchelli, an army chaplain's wife and no feminist at all, had experienced in 1869. She made the trip by "boat, train, steamer, hackery, palkee ghari and pony" from Calcutta arriving in Darjeeling on horseback two months later.

We could have been riding in a palkee ghari, vividly described by this "lady pioneer" in her memoir *The Indian Alps and How We Crossed Them*, as "an oblong deadly-looking machine, resembling a hearse." Happily, we were at least enclosed in the back of a Toyota four-wheel-drive. A dozen young local men gawked curiously as if seeing an American or Canadian tourist for the first time. Two of them rode outside and spat their way through three hours of tall-treed hill country as we climbed higher and higher, stopping only once for chai at Bikky's, an unlikely roadside "hotel & restaurant" on stilts.

We had crisscrossed the narrow tracks of the famed Darjeeling "toy train" as we wound our way to the large, bustling town of Kerseong, but we didn't catch a glimpse of the smoking, oily beast until we reached Ghoom and began our descent into Darjeeling. It might have been the more relaxed way to go, but would have taken eight hours at a pace sometimes slower than a human walk.

Still, as we disgorged from the jeep, exhausted and choking from gas fumes created by heavy traffic, and as dusk turned rapidly to darkness over Darjeeling, I wondered if the lengthier train ride wouldn't have been worth enduring.

The main street was dark except for the odd flickering light. Men huddled in blankets on side streets, struggling to keep warm around wood fires blazing in large barrels. Boys scurried about offering to walk travellers to hotels through the steep switchback streets of this town built on terraces as if to mimic the terraces of the tea estates that have made it famous across the world.

Tired from the journey and still stunned by all the frenetic activity whirling around me, I began to worry that I should never have come all this way. What I didn't know yet was that I had a terrible night ahead in a hotel without running water or central heating,

I slept in my clothes, trying to make my coat provide more warmth than it was capable of doing. Early the next day, I rose before dawn, packed my bag and walked through almost deserted streets to what promised to be a better, if much more expensive, hotel at the highest point of the old city. Once installed, I walked toward a small shop on the way to the market street below.

There I met Pemba Butia, a Tibetan handicraft shop owner. His father, a tailor in the court of the Dalai Lama, sought refuge here even before the Chinese Red Army marched into his homeland in 1949 and well before the 1959 Tibetan uprising against the Chinese occupation. It was then that Darjeeling saw its greatest influx of Tibetans, including Pemba.

"This is a dorje," explained the diminutive Buddhist in remarkably good English for a man with only a Grade 3 education. He was holding a metal thunderbolt in one hand. In the other he demonstrated the high-pitched ring of a set of small cymbals used to call monks to prayer.

"The city is named after the dorje," he continued. "Ling means place, so it is the place of the thunderbolt. That is what they called the old monastery up there." He pointed beyond the Windamere Hotel where I was staying on Observatory Hill.

After hearing that and other stories associated with the many Tibetan curios and religious items in his bathroom-sized shop, I asked Pemba if he would guide me to the Chowk Bazaar, the noisy central market nearby. To my relief, he agreed to do so and promptly closed up shop.

I had visited Old Delhi's Chandni Chowk some days before where I was guided through an endless maze of bazaars by a one-armed Punjabi bicycle rickshaw driver who felt duty bound to show me the underbelly of Old Delhi. He had succeeded, but the intensity of life on the street had exhausted and at times shaken me.

There I found the bazaar and the bizarre: beggars and beggar's daughters, backstreet bakers and chapati makers, spice vendors, nutmeg sorters, chili transporters, outdoor butchers with their bloodied goats' heads swarming with flies, and a turban-clad tea man looking like a giant hooka-smoking caterpillar as he sat atop his Shahi tea sacks. All these Felliniesque images burst forth in the Khari Baoli, a claustrophobic street full of herbs, dried fruits, nuts, even a tree bark used for brushing teeth. It all came at me with a ferocity I had never before experienced and as only India can create.

"We'll be back in about an hour," Pemba told his wife and son in Nepali and we were off down the narrow twisting streets of the city he had lived in for most of his sixty-six years. We walked past two men cleaning duck down by hand and stuffing it into quilts, past another pair with huge doors strapped to their foreheads, past a beautiful young woman sitting on a tea chest on Chatterjee Road.

Finally, we were deep into the Chowk, with Pemba leading me from meat market to spice shop, bead kiosk to fabric seller. Everyone knew him and greeted him warmly. The fruit seller smiled from his sitting position amidst perfectly constructed pyramids of oranges, lemons and green grapes. The tea merchants waved at him, while I snapped photographs of the whole miraculously colourful scene.

We stopped at a tea stall to smell the distinctive aroma of home-grown Darjeeling. The young shop clerk blew her hot breath over a handful of leaves and the full fresh flavour was unleashed. As I would see and taste later, when brewed the leaves would expand to half an inch in diameter and transform into a delicious greenish brown liquid.

A large bowl of yak butter sat at the corner of the counter. Pemba said his wife prepares strong Tibetan tea using the butter and salt each morning for breakfast. But the children find it too strong. They prefer "sugar tea." And though he didn't say it, I know he thought I would too.

On display behind the butter were dozens of hand-packed foil squares colourfully labelled "R.P. Tea Store's First Flush...FTGFOP No. 1." The initials were a mystery to me until Pemba explained that this tea was "Finest Tippy Golden Flowery Orange Pekoe" The "No. 1" meant "First Class," he added. They had been harvested that spring and were selling for forty rupees each.

As we hiked back, I saw the old tea planters' club where the last vestiges of the British Raj are kept virtually embalmed in pristine condition. Here the men who exploited Darjeeling's tea-growing potential drank whisky, played billiards and debated the 1924 Everest expedition. Here they discussed the money they had made transplanting Chinese tea bushes to bring the precious brown tea gold to the tables of the western European public as far back as the 1840s. "Chai?" Pemba offered when we returned to his tiny shop.

"Thanks, but no," I said for I was about to enter the world of those very tea planters to partake of a Darjeeling frozen in time at the Windamere.

The Tibetan Tenduf-La family has owned the hotel since the 1920s and they want it to stay a quaint and comfortable memory of the Raj, explained a family adviser. Early morning "bed tea" and afternoon tea are part of that mystique. And, though they may not quite live up to the strict standards of high tea Raj-style as they did when the Windamere was the private residence of tea planters and indigo growers, they do quite nicely by most other standards.

"It's not a full Victorian Empress tea yet, you understand," said the adviser apologetically. "But the tea is exquisite and is poured out of these wonderful silver pots by a man in a Tibetan headdress." There was no need to apologize. After all, the faded Imperial Hotel in New Delhi, although it has a "Tea Terrace," hardly offers a classic tea like the Windamere does.

"Copper beech and bee-humming lime and ancient mulberry tree cast dappled shade over the tea tables," boasts an advertisement for Lipton's Yellow Label Tea reprinted on the Imperial's menu. The tea tables are neatly set out on the lawns but tea is not served "in the fragile, rose-patterned cups of Spode or Chelsea." And Lipton's bag tea may be "the tea they drink in the Old Country, and in India, and all over the world." But the Windamere of Darjeeling wouldn't be caught dead serving the drying-room-floor dregs that go into most tea bags.

Even the exclusive Rambagh Palace in Jaipur, about three and a half hours by Shatabdi Express train from Delhi, does not live up to Raj standards. You can take afternoon tea on the lawns there and be serenaded by men in orange turbans playing odd stringed instruments and flutes. A man in blue and white checkered headdress will serve you while painted elephants parade on the expansive grounds behind the tearoom. And the Rambagh provides a most comfortable refuge from the din of downtown Jaipur.

But it is at the Windamere that the visitor will enjoy "heavenly Darjeeling tea sipped at dawn while the Kanchenjunga turns from glimmering pink to remote white," as the hotel's brochure enthuses. It is there that you will see "marigolds at the dining table, brisk waiters in elaborate, peaked turbans and the room full of light." And "most of all," in the syrupy words of the brochure, it is at the Windamere that "you will clutch your dream tightly because you will remember that the mountains and you were young together."

They would soon be adding fresh-baked scones and clotted cream to their afternoon tea menu, the adviser assured me. But I was already convinced that the Windamere is permanently imbued with the stuff of greatness. Here was a hill station tea with real class!

Tea at the Top of the World (Part II)
A pilgrimage to the Mecca of tea

The dawn mist was silently lifting from the tea-covered green hills that surround Darjeeling and, as the early morning sun sparkled through the mist, I could see two of the five snow-capped peaks of Mount Kanchenjunga, the third highest mountain on earth (28,208 feet) as I looked through my sitting room window. It was late February, the coolish off-season for tea producers and tea tourists alike, and I was lingering in my warm bed at the Windamere Hotel, a "Heritage Inn of the Himalayas" in West Bengal, India.

By 8 a.m., I had enjoyed a full English breakfast with a steaming cup of coffee from the Baba Budan Hills. Another western traveller glared as if to scold me for not indulging in a pot of pale Darjeeling tea. But I was in no hurry. I would drink my fill of the hotel's own "private stock of tea...served by the fire in the sitting room...since 1939." And I would indulge in other tea fancies as well during my stay here.

Like the tea, the hotel is "an original," says its twenty-four-page brochure. Room No. 3 of twenty-seven rooms was equipped with a blazing coal fireplace. Its tiny sitting room overlooked snowy peaks that seemed close enough to touch. As I gazed out for some reason I thought of Coleridge's *Rime of the Ancient Mariner* line, as idle as a painted ship upon a painted ocean. The imagery was similar.

I emerged from the semi-trance and looked back at my little cottage with its "chain-action water closet" that had "been giving dependable service since 1912." That was welcome news.

Pemba Butia, my Tibet tea guide and
companion in Darjeeling, India.

Thankfully I had found a fabulously warm refuge in the heart of the Himalayas. The night before I had nearly frozen to death in a lesser hotel down the road. Now, the Windamere, the only "inn of distinction" in Darjeeling, was my temporary home. It was also the most expensive at $70-$80 U.S. (single occupancy), but what I was about to get for the money was a priceless memory that refuses to fade even today.

"In the face of all this dreary uniformity," the brochure went on, "the hotel has simply stood still and elbowed change away with a gentle insistence." That includes continuing to warm your room with a hot fire and your bed with a bronze warming pan.

No need to ask for a room with a view at the Windamere, counsels the brochure. "Every window looks out at mist-dappled aspects, riveting foliage in enraptured, bouncing swashes of green and blinding peaks that form ladders from earth to heaven and back again." It was such poetic truth.

***

After being served "bed tea" and later a hearty breakfast, I wandered over to the Chowrasta or central square just outside the gates of the Windamere. Uniformed school children were skipping happily. A young woman idly swept the streets with a hand broom, while a legless beggar bobbed along behind her using two wooden blocks as hand stilts. Men with ponies for hire waited for the daytime crowds. A statue of Nepal's national poet watched over the scene near the entrance to Observatory Hill where an old Buddhist monastery once stood.

The Oxford bookstore, with its fine collection of rare tea books and hundred-rupee packages of local tea, was not yet open. Yet more men stood nearby drinking glasses of steaming hot chai. It might have been pure Darjeeling, but they were probably drinking an inferior leaf – the dross from the green gold that keeps the boomtown-like city of 140,000 alive and relatively well off.

A few days earlier, I had seen the chaiwallahs (street tea sellers) of Delhi brewing their concoctions in the narrow passageways of the Chandni Chowk, a notoriously bustling part of Old Delhi which is so disarming to western sensibilities and so culturally chaotic that it takes some travellers something much more potent than a cup of tea to get over their first visit.

I had been warned away from the street tea by my bicycle rickshaw guide, a one-armed Punjabi man named Rakesh. "Not good quality tea," he scowled. Heeding his advice had probably forestalled a mild case of Delhi Belly (gastroenteritis), an affliction that many travellers suffer sooner or later in India.

My new Punjabi friend was so insistent on helping me avoid that misery that I wasn't able to risk tasting the milky sweet mixture until a few days later when I commissioned an auto-rickshaw driver in Jaipur to drive me to his favourite chaiwallah's stall.

As the Jaipur tea seller brewed my cuppa in a battered pot on an equally beat-up portable stove, my driver explained the procedure. "He boils the water and tosses the tea into it, you see." I did see, of course, but wondered about the other ingredients. "That is lichee," the driver said as the chaiwallah crushed a large cardamon seed under a spoon and dumped it into the battered metal saucepan. I also tasted another ingredient as we sipped from small, hot glasses. "Yes, that is ginger," said the driver. "It is used only in winter because it warms and refreshes us."

Recalling the delicious taste, I considered taking a glass with the men across the Chowrasta. Heaven knows it was cool enough and the glass would have warmed my hands. But the painful memory of a previous bout of Delhi Belly brought me to my senses. Turning, I caught another fleeting glimpse of omnipresent Kanchenjunga before walking down into the crowded city to see for myself where the world's best-known tea is harvested and produced for export to anxious teetotallers all over the globe.

I was anxious to walk through one of the nearby tea estates that form a bumpy but carefully woven quilt of green all around Darjeeling. The closest one is Happy Valley a few kilometres away from the Chowk Bazaar where street traders compete with tour operators to see who can make the most noise. The walk took me past the Catholic Church, Loreto Convent and that most officious of monuments to the British Raj, the District Magistrate's Office.

When I arrived, the estate itself was dormant, as were most of them at that time of year. They would come to life again when the first spring flush of tea was ready for plucking. The current solitude was a merciful change from the cacophony of the Chowk.

Children playing with newborn pups paid me no attention as I stumbled along the steep cobbled trail deeper into the terraces of the estate. Workers were too busy to notice me as they hoisted heavy loads of hay and tea-bush clippings onto their foreheads. Grand-mothers busily hung laundry in the crisp sunny air while their daughters-in-law tended babies and fed chickens.

Nearby, an old woman plucked dead leaves from the bushes as she has done for a lifetime. Her head was wrapped in a shawl; a large ring was inserted in her nose. She was as much a fixture here as the ancient camellia sinensis plants themselves.

The tea-producing machinery remained idle in the cool interior of the main building. It had been washed down and repainted recently to await the spring season. If I wanted to see a real tea-producing operation I would have to visit Maikabari Tea Estate.

To get there I hired a little red van and driver for the exorbitant fee of 650 rupees, thus putting my life in his hands as we careened down a narrow side road outside of Kerseong, leading us past Castleton Tea Estate with its "Tea Research Centre." At times, the driver came so close to oncoming traffic that I pulled my hand away from the open window for fear of getting clipped. Finally, after much stopping and starting, honking and backing up along the tiny roadway, we arrived.

Nina Mazuchelli would no doubt have found the estate "eminently unpicturesque." That's how she described tea plantations in her 1876 memoir *The Indian Alps and How We Crossed Them*. "Only interesting...to the eye of the planter," she complained. They have "the unromantic appearance of an exaggerated cabbage garden."

The "lady pioneer," a professed "tea-lover" and wife of an army chaplain posted to Darjeeling, "half regretted having witnessed the process of manufacturing the 'cup that cheers'." But I was captivated by the beauty of Makaibari and anxious to learn about its workings.

"Darjeeling teas are known for their mellowness," said Vikras Khatyra, the lead hand who met me at the entrance. "Assam teas are known for their bitterness," he added as he began to work his way methodically through the various tea-producing processes: plucking, withering, rolling, sifting, fermenting, drying, sorting, testing, and packing.

Slowly, he ran through all the secrets that the old tea planters of the British Raj had used to make the "fine tippy golden flowery orange pekoe" that is the cream of Makaibari's 100,000-kilo annual crop.

Vikras's detailed explanations had partially satisfied my curiosity as the van pulled away and sped along the same narrow road down into the valley where Makaibari finally ends and Longview Tea Estate begins.

Along the way, tea workers prepared for the coming spring flush. People congregated around the single water tap at the centre of tea workers' villages. Women washed their hair and men brushed their teeth while little goats wandered freely as children played among the grass huts they call home.

By early March, the quiet of the off-season here would end. The villagers would head for the tea gardens and the freshly painted silver and green machines at Makaibari would again whir to life to begin the process of bringing "Pure Darjeeling" to markets the world over.

***

Breathing shorter and shorter breaths of thin Himalayan air had made me hungry, so I was grateful for the Windamere's unique, piano-accompanied afternoon tea at 4 p.m. Tomato sandwiches, shortbread and currant cakes were the fare and tea was liberally poured until the piano music gave way to a Nepalese folk-singing group.

By 5 p.m., the tea things were cleared away, making room in the fireplace-warmed Bear's Park Parlour for gin and tonic and some Indian snacks, featuring chicken tikka.

With this abundance of good things before me, I had all but forgotten about how my visit began with frozen limbs, open street fires and a hopeless lost feeling. Ensconced in what the Windamere brochure calls this "mellow Edwardian dream reminiscent of a lost world," the dinner gong brought me back to the new world at 7 p.m. sharp.

As I left the parlour, I spotted a poem hanging in the gallery of old photographs and paintings. It said as follows:

"As the glow of Kanchenjunga fades
with the passing of each year
And the whistle of the toy train dies
at last upon my ear
In my heart I still shall cherish
dear old Windamere."

It was signed by the renowned Welsh travel writer Jan Morris on a visit to this "tiny trinket of a town" in January 1996.

More interested in my stomach than my heart, I ambled toward the circular end of the dining hall where a very English-sounding "Dilled beet soup" was being served, followed by a choice of "Shepherd's Pie with mixed baby greens" or several delicious-sounding Tibetan dishes. I had it all, finishing with the best cup of tea imaginable.

The tea dining would begin again early the next day with more bed tea and a hearty full-fry English breakfast. My pilgrimage to the place that tea built was starting to show around my middle and my heart had started to share Jan Morris's sentiment.

Tea in the 'Whore of the Orient'
The best little teahouse in Shanghai

Mr. Wong was an impatient driver. I didn't know exactly what he was shouting to the other drivers on the crowded streets of Shanghai. Mr. Shen, our trusty private tour guide, grimaced which seemed to indicate that whatever Mr. Wong was yelling, it must have been in a forbidden language, the kind one might have expected from sailors.

Tea being served at the the Mid-Lake Pavilion Teahouse in Shanghai's Yu Gardens.

Mr. Shen glanced over at Mr. Wong as if to warn him that his behaviour was attracting notice. The guide was intent on leaving a good impression on his clients. Indeed, his eagerness to please might have suggested that he was sworn to it by higher powers in Beijing.

Mr. Wong looked across at Mr. Shen and nodded. He had seen tourists – and sailors – come in search of fulfilment for their wildest fantasies during a layover in the 'Whore of the Orient.' My fantasy was less prurient. I simply wanted to visit the famed Yuyuan Gardens (Yu Gardens for short) and indulge my passion for tea at the Mid-Lake Pavilion Teahouse perched magisterially at the entrance to the ancient gardens.

As our devoted guide, Mr. Shen felt he should apologize for Mr. Wong's apparently filthy tongue and general bad manners. I was none the wiser, of course, since I spoke at most four words of Mandarin or Cantonese, I wasn't sure which. And Mr. Wong was not about to stop cursing the thousands of bicyclists who had the misfortune to cross his line of vision or worse the trajectory of his mercifully air-conditioned Honda Accord.

He had just dropped us at a 'tourist restaurant' where we were about to dine on the usual array of foods, all converging on our table at once. Our view of the harbour was exquisite. When we didn't have half a dozen servers hovering near us, we could see dozens of construction cranes on the horizon along the Huangpu River. They were erecting high-rise office towers and new housing so quickly that the buildings seemed to grow instantaneously as I watched. The old city was being imploded to make room for the new capitalism of Deng Xiaoping, Mao's aging replacement.

Hovels with laundry dangling from open windows sat waiting for construction crews to erect bamboo scaffolding, the Bamboo Curtain of the 1990s, so yet another building could go up in their place. Itinerant labourers live – sleep, eat, drink endless pots of tea – on site under cover of materials waiting to be used. When Rudyard Kipling said East and West would never meet he hadn't seen today's Shanghai. These days they are meeting and the results are both miraculous and frightening.

As I gazed dreamily out the restaurant's broad window panels, Mr. Shen urged me to finish my meal quickly. We must be off before the Yu Gardens closed. We wouldn't want to miss the very special afternoon tea he had promised.

We entered the teahouse and were immediately escorted upstairs. Out on the bustling street, Mr. Wong leaned against his Accord, taking a long leisurely pull on a canning jar full of a foul-looking liquid which appeared to have worms wriggling in it. Mr. Shen explained that it was tea or a concoction that included tea. I was learning that this is standard equipment for taxi drivers in China.

Mr. Wong gave us an angry, impatient look, but kindly opened the taxi door and gestured for us to re-board the Accord. We were ready for our adventure to the Yu Gardens teahouse, a pleasure that was denied many Chinese during the Cultural Revolution when teahouses were seen as decadent and everything old was marked for destruction by the young Red Guards.

For an entire generation, school was out, not for the summer, but for a decade. And the chance to experience a part of their country's history at the old tearoom was lost. I was about to have what they had missed or forsaken since the 1970s.

Mr. Wong brought the Accord to a jerky halt and we stepped into the heat to wander through a market in the old Shanghai. "Must go now, must hurry," Mr. Shen insisted. "Teahouse close soon." We stepped up our pace and rounded a narrow street corner that fed into a square with a peaceful pond as its centrepiece. Strange, zigzagging whitewashed walkways stretched across the water, leading to a two-storey pagoda-like structure.

Mr. Shen stopped, turned to me and smiled proudly. This was the teahouse we'd been waiting for. Sitting on stilts, its carved roof peaks, grey tiles and fire-engine-red window frames sparkled in the afternoon Shanghai sun.

In Mandarin it is called the Hu Xin Ting (lake heart pavilion). It is the oldest operating teahouse in Shanghai. A Ming Dynasty bureaucrat named Pan Yunduan originally built it as part of a private garden for his parents. In 1784 some Qing Dynasty textile merchants donated money to renovate and extend the structure.

It became a public teahouse in 1855 and since then "through good or bad and the changing of management, for the past 140 years, it has never stopped serving tea," said a brochure. "Even Queen Elizabeth couldn't resist the temptation to come sip at the heart of a lake, and just for a moment become a Chinese Queen!"

Shanghai residents appeared to be enjoying the warm sun at plain tables and chairs on the main floor. The second floor was reserved for foreign visitors and the polished mahogany furniture, hanging lanterns, black and white Chinese paintings and teapot displays were definitely meant to impress even the most royal of guests.

We took a small table by a windowed alcove overlooking the pond and surrounding buildings. The beauty and tranquillity of the setting made it the perfect place to enjoy tea. We ordered both jasmine and black tea "made from pure mineral water and from delicate tea leaves produced in different famous tea-growing areas." Then I sat back to soak up the view both outside and in.

Our tea came quickly, the jasmine served in a covered cup and the black in a brown clay pot accompanied by a much smaller cup. It was followed by a small platter of tiny hard-boiled quail eggs ("tea quail eggs," according to the menu), equally tiny tofu squares, preserved plums wrapped in plastic like candy, and delicious sticky rice with tender pork buried at its centre and bound neatly and tightly with thin string in a small green leaf.

I was smitten by the care with which everything was arranged and served, tea nonplussed by it all. To finish me off, a young woman presented me with a Chinese fan which had printed on it a colourful image of the memorable teahouse. If tea lovers go to heaven, I concluded, this is what it might be like. And heaven came at a cost of 25 yuan each (about $4).

Mr. Wong was taking a long pull on his canning jar when we returned from our tea and a tour of the lovely Yu Gardens with their incredible rock formations, trees, statutes and flowers. He was smiling beatifically and looked a tiny bit Buddha-like. I suspected that the concoction might have included more than a little sake or something even stronger. It certainly wasn't tea alone in that jar.

Mr. Shen shared my suspicion with a roll of his eyes, but he said nothing as we drove toward another one of the many splendours of this mysterious Paris of the Orient.

Tea and madness at Raffles
Where Conrad, Kipling and Noel Coward took their 'tiffin'

About an hour out of Singapore on the seven-hour train trip from Kuala Lumpur which was located higher up and to the northwest on the Malaysian peninsula, I began to question my motivation for visiting a modern city state where gum-chewing is forbidden, American boys are caned and Filipina maids are executed.

My sole intention was to have afternoon tea at Raffles, one of the world's poshest hotels (cheap rooms: $650). But to some, coming three-quarters of the way around the world for a cup of tea might have seemed a clear sign of oncoming madness.

I was on my second cup of Lipton's as we passed through Johor Bahru, a city just across the Straits of Johore described as 'bussling' by my guide book. They took my Malaysia entry card there and I sat back while the train transported me from East to West, from Third World to First World, in a matter of minutes.

The opulence of Raffles was not far away now, but the Singapore train station was a far cry from the spotless metropolis I had expected. It was rather dingy and well past its time. The underground metro was the opposite: a modern, efficient, clinically clean service. I was at my stop in a few minutes and after a short walk stood staring at the great white queen of the East.

Here was half a city block that represented not a hotel but a conquering imperial power, a symbol of the island jewel that Sir Stamford Raffles, like some British conquistador, had claimed for Queen Victoria and turned into another Crown colony to add to her vast empire.

"Is this where they serve the famous tea?" I asked the clerk who was peering at me over her half-spectacles. "I've come a very long way to take tea at your world-renowned Tiffin Room, so I hope you can squeeze me in somewhere." More peering until finally a young waiter whispered that there was a spot near the exit that might be suitable for a western tea tourist.

He took my umbrella and escorted me through to the Tiffin Room, just opposite the Writer's Bar, and seated me facing the most amazing crowd of teacup-tinkling, trifle-tasting, Breakfast-at-Tiffany's post-Victorians I'd ever seen. But for the modern dress, it might have been the same crowd that populated the short stories in Somerset Maugham's *The Casuarina Tree*, a book set on the Malay peninsula long before Singapore had broken away from the Federated Malay States, now called Malaysia.

To my back was a display of savoury dishes steaming with delectable fare on a long table and two side tables were draped in mouth-watering desserts. Above the long table was a large mirror with 'Tiffin Room' engraved on it. Tiffin is defined in the Oxford English Dictionary as a meal of light curries with chutney but is sometimes used to describe afternoon tea.

Raffles was first opened on December 1, 1887, by the Sarkies Brothers, and was soon welcoming the likes of famed writers like Joseph Conrad, Rudyard Kipling and Noel Coward. Kipling learned to love curries and chutneys in the Tiffin Room. "Feed at Raffles," he once wrote, "and sleep at the Hotel de l'Europe." His Sunday afternoon meals began a tradition called Sunday Tiffin, according to my main waiter Desmond Goh. He began working at Raffles in 1991 and is a devoted Rafflesian.

I was there in the midst of such literary history to take my afternoon tea, curry included, and what a tea it was! The table before me was covered in snow-white linen. The Gainsborough silverware lay on a starched-stiff white napkin the size of a small sheet. A heavy polished-silver sugar bowl and creamer sat next to a single mauve orchid perched in a shiny metal vase.

My tea came loose in metal with a silver strainer and catcher. The small pot carried the label, English Breakfast, and its handle was covered with a dainty white holder to protect the pouring hand. The cup, saucer and plates were specially made for Raffles by Royal Doulton. And, of course, everything carried the distinctive Raffles insignia.

This is the wealth of detail that must have caused the late Canadian man of letters George Woodcock to remark on "the antique splendour of Raffles." It must also have soothed the author of the 1960s book *Anarchism* for Raffles was nothing if not meticulously well-ordered and anti-anarchistic.

There were ladies in floral print dresses with proper British accents, young couples gazing lovingly into one another's eyes, retirees on their dream vacations, all races but mostly white Westerners. They were all being fussed over by an army of men of colour dressed in white cotton who were anxious to fill half-empty teacups or clear half-full plates to make room for yet another culinary indulgence made to perfection for the discerning and usually very rich Raffles clientele. This tea traveller was the exception.

How varied, culturally diverse and sinfully delightful were those indulgences: quiches galore, dim sum with steamed pork buns, noodles and pastries full of meat, fish and vegetables, mini-bagels covered in cream cheese with a pecan for a bonnet. And, of course, the usual tea sandwiches, perfectly shaped and displayed crust-free in their abundance.

Hot dishes, cold dishes, gourmet platters prepared on the spot, foods for every taste. It went on endlessly this cornucopia of edible delights. When you tired of the savoury dishes it was time to move on to the sweet ones: mousses and custards, cakes oozing cream and exotic fruits perfectly arranged, squares and scones. Every devilish taste imaginable was a beckoning temptation, a tea traveller's dream, a dieter's nightmare.

Above me, the big fans moved silently on the high ceilings between chandeliers in the shape of giant scallop shells held together by the golden stems of metal roses. Coloured drawings of tropical plants and flowers lined the walls. To my right, great white-arched glass doors opened revealing a massive green fountain and statue straddled by two massive palms.

This was Victoriana at its most magnificent and its most decadent brought back to life in the 1990s all spit and polish and at your service, sir and madam. What a place it must have been when Conrad, Jack London and Maugham roamed the South Pacific in search of inspiration for their short stories and local tales to spice up high-seas adventures like London's *The Sea Wolf* and Conrad's *Lord Jim.* Conrad might even have begun plotting his masterpiece *Heart of Darkness* here in this very room, I thought.

I drank in great gulpfuls of the ambience and history as two, sometimes three waiters made sure my teapot was always filled with freshly brewed Assam or Darjeeling picked from a choice of dozens of other fine teas. Finally, I called a halt, paid the bill, a budget-busting $24 plus tip, and moved off to the Raffles shop.

The shop went on for three rooms and there one could buy artefacts of that ambience and history at hugely inflated prices. Kimonos, shirts, ties, jackets, towels, bath robes silverware, tea cups and the like all with the Raffles imprimatur that seemed to shout 'I've taken tea at one of the world's most exquisite tearooms.'

An hour later I escaped with a paltry $50 in souvenirs and several priceless memories. Quite sated I managed to climb some nearby steps to another Raffles institution, the Long Bar, where I capped off the afternoon with a Singapore Sling. Not just any Singapore Sling, mind you, but THE Singapore Sling. Raffles is reputed to be where the cocktail was invented.

The whole affair had been a grand adventure not easily topped, certainly not by a later trip to the Singapore zoo where I was promised afternoon tea with an orang-utan. Alas, it didn't quite live up to its billing. Mithra, as the hairy beast was called, had no intention of taking tea with anyone least of all a tea-sogged Canadian.

I was guided to a stump in a nearby garden, given a cup of bagged tea and left to watch Mithra grunt between bites of the hairy fruit, rambutan, and smelly handfuls of the king of all fruits, durian.

She deigned to pause briefly to pose for a photograph so I could brag that I had taken tea with an ape.

It was an over-rated experience but I suppose it should confirm that I am totally mad...about tea anyway!

The Purple Cane of Kuala Lumpur
The perfect setting for a Somerset Maugham story

Kuala Lumpur is a welcome refuge from the twenty-four-hour non-stop madhouse of Bangkok. There is still an endless flow of noisy traffic pumping gas fumes that choke passing pedestrians. Taxi drivers will cheat you here almost as innocently as they do in Thailand. Slick-haired, smooth-talking touts are less conspicuous but they, like the Thai versions, will sidle up to you to display pictures of their sisters, mothers and little brothers. And there is always the relentless heat.

But little KL – about a tenth the size of Bangkok – is somehow quieter, more civilized. The trappings of empire are still to be found here, among them tea, and that is what brought me to the thriving capital of Malaysia (population one million).

Back in the 1920s, British tea companies started testing soil in the Cameron Highlands and by 1933 had set up a full-production tea plantation with plenty of year-round cheap labour, according to legendary tea historian William Ukers. The Chinese got into the act, too, and began selling green tea to labourers in the tin mines of the region. So tea has been a lucrative trade here for decades.

I hopped the No. 7 bus into KL from the airport. When the driver told me to get off I thought he had mistaken the old train station for an ancient mosque. It was gorgeous. A few blocks away I noticed the National Mosque with its odd angles, stairways, tall *obelisque* and generous carefully manicured grounds. I soon learned that the Malaysian capital is as earnestly Muslim as Bangkok is Buddhist.

KL is a cleaner city than Bangkok, proud of its Muslim heritage and anxious to shed any lingering British colonial habits. In Merdaka Square, a four-foot-thick flagpole holds high a huge fluttering Malaysian flag, a symbol of the country's independence from Britain in the late 1950s.

A worker changed a light bulb as I snapped a shot of 'Big Ben', the clock tower in the Sultan Abd Samad Building, a superb example of Moorish architecture which now houses the Supreme Court and is probably the best known building in the city.

I continued walking through rush-hour traffic until I arrived at Jalan Bukit Bitang. There, in the basement of the BB Plaza, the first shopping centre in KL, was the Rasa Utara restaurant, specializing in traditional Malaysian dishes. No alcohol is served, but of course there's plenty of tea.

I ordered a deliciously light chicken curry served with a 'net' pancake. Indeed, the yellow folded crepe looked just like a net. The dish included spicy anchovies and a root vegetable cooked with ginger. Some steamed rice and an almost tasteless star fruit juice complemented the main course. For desert I couldn't resist having a "mango tango" ice cream cone at the neighbouring Baskin and Robbins, a modern American invader that seemed incongruous in these surroundings.

Later I would sample the satays for which Malaysians are so famous at Satay Anika, one of KL's older restaurants and a bit too much of a fast-food operation when I visited. The curry had given me a craving for tea.

I eventually convinced a cabbie to take me to the Central Market, a building full of crafts, food stalls and pubs selling Anchor, a passable Malaysian lager. As we drove, the driver admitted unashamedly that the ten ringit he was charging me was at least double what the official fare would have been. A dollar bought you 1.76 RM back then.

A short walk from the market, in the heart of KL's Chinatown, up on a second floor in Jalan Panggong, a neon sign beckoned passers-by to enjoy tea at the Purple Cane Teahouse. The tearoom itself was on the third floor. On the second floor, they sold Chinese teas imported from Suzhou, Fujian province and Hunan province. Oolong, Keemun, Jasmine and several others were all lined up in

My tea server and guide at the Purple Cane n Kuala Lumpur.

pretty containers. Also on display were brick tea, loose tea, tea bags, tea-making utensils and teapots of all sizes and varieties.

Upstairs, the tearoom offered both a traditional tea-drinking area, where sippers were seated on the floor, or one with tables and chairs for those of us who prefer to take our tea sitting upright. I chose the latter and ordered a pot of "rose peony tea." My tea table included a heating device on which had been placed a small metal kettle.

"It is slow-burning," explained a young man who on seeing my look of uncertainty had offered to assist me. Tea making is a delicate and precise process for the Chinese, and the Purple Cane was determined to provide KL with an authentic Chinese tea-drinking experience.

"Important to heat water slowly," my Malaysian helper said. Using good water is equally important, he added, starting to shift into lecture mode. He dwelled on his subject in broken but reasonably good English, making sure that I knew he knew what he was talking about when it came to Chinese tea.

"Must be very hot," he stressed again, admonishing me for pouring the water over my tea too early. He had been reading a new book called *All the Tea in China* and was anxious to tell of its secrets. He found the chapter on early Chinese tearooms fascinating. "Tearoom is place of conviviality and quiet bustle," he read from the book, having difficulty with the word conviviality.

The old Chinese teahouses upon which the Purple Cane modelled itself, were places "where people with very little money could still enjoy entertainment," he read on. Then he paused to show me a poster announcing a poetry reading at the Cane later that week. I looked at him to show that I was impressed.

The old teahouses also thrived on gambling, prostitution and other shady activities, some of which are described in a famous Lao She play called *The Teahouse*, according to the book. But these days, a tearoom like the Cane is more likely to entertain young business entrepreneurs and lovers in search of a quiet conversation than it is gangsters.

An old-style teahouse named after Lao She had opened in Beijing, my helper explained. It offered drum music and work by traditional folk artists. He intended that the Cane would emulate it as much as was possible.

We began our tea making once again. This time it would be done properly. He poured this time, dousing the whole array of ceramic and porcelain implements that were sitting on a circular clay stand. The freshly boiled water quickly drained into the hollow base of the stand, leaving everything steaming hot and clean. He then filled my cup to just the right level, making the colourful rose-peony mixture swirl and tumble. Then gently he set the cover over the cup. The whole process was partly precise art form and partly Chinese tea ritual.

"Ouch!" I winced when my fingers touched the large covered cup in which the tea was brewing, another traditional Chinese method. It was too hot for me so my Cane host quickly emptied it into an open creamer-like container to cool, then finally into a cup not much bigger than a thimble. It was an exquisite tasting brew. The cost: about $1.50.

The Purple Cane had been in business for nine years in October 1995 and was one of only a few authentic Chinese tearooms still operating in KL, my helper said. He had worked in the second-floor shop for about a year and now wanted to expand his knowledge of tea ceremonies and serving rituals.

As I travelled in the Asia-Pacific region, I had been reading Somerset Maugham stories. The British author of *The Razor's Edge*, *Of Human Bondage* and so many memorable plays and short stories might have liked the Purple Cane, I thought. He might have welcomed its tranquil atmosphere as I had relished the escape from KL's intensity. He most certainly would have approved of its commitment to fine tea and ancient tea traditions.

The Purple Cane, with its dark corners hidden by beaded curtains, suggested the possibility of sinister goings-on which would have appealed. The fiction writer might envisage plots being hatched in whispered tones behind those curtains. It might even have inspired one of the many stories Maugham set in this culturally puzzling yet ever-fascinating part of the world. In fact, it could have been the perfect setting for a murder mystery...or a love story.

Tea Tranquility in Hong Kong
In the time before teapots were invented

Hong Kong, like so much of Asia, is a place of converging and contrasting cultures. It`s all there: the ubiquitous mobile phones that the kids holster like six-guns, the oceans of neon along Nathan Road in Kowloon, the double-decker buses that serve as reminders of a time when the sun never set on British Empire.

This mini-Manhattan that is ever more tightly squeezed onto HK Island had all the amenities that westerners often insist that their destinations offer. The Accidental Tourist could even find his or her favourite fast-food chain here. But nothing seemed to quite fit.

I was contemplating all of this over a glass of tea coloured with Carnation canned milk and a tasteless lunch that was ordered as an omelette but arrived as an egg sandwich at the Hillwood Snack Bar. With that incongruity in mind, the reader will see what I mean about cultures not quite fitting together properly.

My plan was to ride the famed Star Ferry, the cheapest thing in HK at about 35 cents a trip. I might have had afternoon tea on the bobbing green and yellow passenger ferry, but my timing was wrong. It was well past tea time so I would have to enjoy the famous Victoria Harbour view tea-less. The shiny bank towers thrusting toward the sky contrasted with so much of HK that remained Chinese in spite of the British.

Once off the ferry, I made for Hong Kong Park, a gorgeous green oasis in the concrete jungle that six million people called home. Here turtles sunned themselves with their back legs stretched out lazily on a giant lily pad shaped like a canapé tray. Fish wove among the floating flowers and birds fluttered in the forested areas above.

Within the oasis was the Flagstaff House Museum of Teaware, perhaps another incongruity in this tiny island empire. Inside I surveyed the old Greek Revival-style Headquarter House, home of the Commander in Chief of British Forces in HK since 1846. It offered the welcome solace and quiet of a cathedral while only a few blocks away HK rocked and tumbled along.

"Selected Works of Chinese Tea Ware from the K.S. Lo Collection" was the title of the display on view and I was swept off my feet by the delicacy of these antiquities. Every phase of tea drinking was depicted dating from before the Tang and Song dynasties when tea started to flourish as a refreshing drink.

I was awed by the early vessels or ewers which carried tea in the pre-teapot eleventh and twelfth centuries when tea was thought of as a medicine and tea leaves were cooked with ginger, leeks and other vegetables. Tea utensils, I learned, were not essential in those early years since tea was taken as a healing broth in ordinary household receptacles.

Changsha ewers without spouts were prominent. It took several dynasties for the ewer to grow a proper spout, but eventually it evolved into the world's first teapot as we know them. It was during the Five Dynasties, though, that the Tang design was greatly improved by the addition of a longer spout.

For teaware lovers, the museum is a candy store full of goodies. Perhaps the most stunning is the snow-white Dehua porcelain teapot with its moulded red and brown top. It's a treasure from the late Ming to early Qing dynasties.

Then there are the *famille-rose* and *famille noire* styles of teaware, the adorable Yingqing glazed cups and saucers and the very special collection of *famille-verte* cups. Out of the six hundred pieces contributed by K.S. Lo, a viewing of the museum video revealed that these twelve cups, with their colourful floral designs representing the months of the year, were his obvious favourites.

On the museum walls were depicted the various methods of making tea through the ages. Powdered tea added to boiling salt water was recommended by Tang dynasty tea connoisseur Lu Wu in his classic tea book, *Chajing.* Whipped tea was common during the Song dynasty, where a concoction of tea powder was whipped into a froth with a bamboo whisk. Tea drinkers of the Ming dynasty preferred steamed tea where washing the leaves is required. Finally, Gongfu tea, popular in the tea-growing province of Fujian in China, is said to be the best way to prepare Oolong tea.

The contrast of rampant development outside with these intricate, thoughtful age-old methods of making and drinking tea inside seemed an amazing contradiction. I pondered it and, having viewed the many tea-making methods, I also began to crave a cup of the world's oldest hot beverage.

Unfortunately none was to be had at the museum, at least not then. So I set my course for the Luk Yu Teahouse Stanley Street. It was established in 925 A.D. and was still going strong more than a thousand years later.

Luk Yu, by the way, was a Tang dynasty politician who, "disenchanted by the internal strife and widespread corruption amongst government officials, quit politics and devoted himself wholeheartedly to the study of tea." There was even a statue of the old boy on the second floor of the five-hundred-seat teahouse.

My guidebook called it "a temple to the morning ritual of drinking tea with dim sum," adding that it was also becoming notorious because it had been the site of a recent triad shooting. When I entered, it had the look of a Hollywood set for a gangster movie, with its old-style wooden booths, mirrored cupboards and brass spittoons.

Still, there was a decided charm about the place and I soon learned why it is so popular. The tea was a secret potion that was to die for. Not literally, of course; we'll leave that to the movie gangsters. But it was a delectable treat exquisitely brewed with all the key qualities associated with tea: it cooled the body while refreshing it. It was the pick-me-up that tea advertisements brag about.

I asked about purchasing some of the loose leaves after going through several cups between bites of deep-fried shrimp pastry, pork balls, a giant steamed chicken bun and more shrimp wrapped in noodles. I was told I could but one packet would cost about $3. For some reason, the waiter insisted that we "must use whole packet for one pot."

I declined and instead visited the Chan Chun Lan Tea Shop (established in 1855) on nearby Cochrane Street. Here I found three elderly men waiting to serve me a tea world version of Linkin', Blinkin' and Nod. They were not in a hurry. They did not carry cellular phones on their hips, as did the construction workers across the way. They did not urge me to buy or smell or taste, as they do in the fish market, fruit and vegetable stalls, and endless clothing cubby holes down around the Li Yuen market alleyways.

I spoke about as much Cantonese as the three old tea merchants spoke English, so this transaction would be done by smell and finger pointing and by ooos and ahhs. The Spring Bud Jasmine smelled divine and just to prove that it was, one merchant instructed another to open a large jar of the lesser Jasmine.

Oh yes. Please, pretty please! Sell me a can, no, make it three canisters full of the Spring Bud. To me, to any tea lover, it was as precious as a cargo of opium clandestinely purchased somewhere in the bustling heart of this tiny bundle of contradictions racing to its destiny with mainland China.

Tea in the Land of Living Dangerously
Tea pluckers rushed at me like a symphony of angry swans

In pre-tsunami times, and even now I suppose, middle-class Indonesians spend their holidays in the resort towns of Central Java about sixty kilometres south of Jakarta near Bogor with its famous botanical gardens. I had come for a different reason: the search for some of Indonesia's finest leaf tea at the Golden Mountain Tea Estate at Cisarua.

Triangular stacks of fresh-picked fruit and vegetables sat by the roadside as Parminto (a.k.a. Johnny) drove the empty tourist van through Ciawi, Cibogo, Cipayung and other hill towns. High into the surrounding mountains, the villages gave way to tea country demarcated partly by huge red irises along the winding road.

The bright red flowers contrasted with the blue plastic roofs of the endless warungs (stalls) mostly selling corn on the cob. The scene was completed by the colourful costumes and wide-brimmed hats of the tea pluckers roaming through the green jigsaw-shaped tea gardens.

I had seen a similar image of pastoral Asian bliss a few days before in paintings on the bottom of bird cages hanging from the ceiling of the Café Batavia in the old Dutch colonial section of Jakarta. It seemed a romantic image of tranquility and peace frozen in time. Now it was rudely interrupted when I suddenly shouted "Stop!" to Johnny.

The young driver hit the brakes and I quickly jumped from the van and wandered toward the pluckers excitedly hoping that I would snap the perfect tea worker photograph. When I set foot in the gardens, the lot of them – about fifteen – rushed towards me herd-like, kicking their long skirts out of the way or holding them up as they rustled through the tea plants.

I took a few steps further into the gardens still hopeful but the idyllic image began to transform into something real and imperfect and even threatening. As the pluckers got closer, I saw their sweaty red foreheads as they pushed back their hats. As they peeled off their gloves, their hands were permanently stained with tea tattoos. They had rips in their skirts from the sharp edges of the tea bushes so that what seemed like costumes worthy of a Broadway musical based on tea were now merely baggy work clothes.

These were hard workers and they smelled the smell of money when they saw me coming. Soon they swarmed me. "Take picture, mister. Take picture," one shouted. Another held out her hand and made the finger motions for payment. I clicked and flashed twice, then threw a 5,000-rupiah note at the foot of the tea rabble that was now forming in front of me.

I didn't dare look back as I walked briskly back to the waiting van. There was a great uproar behind me as the pluckers clucked and cackled, scolding me for drawing them out of the fields, away from their work, and then failing to adequately compensate each of them.

Johnny revved the engine and Daniel, my guide and the only other rider, gave him the signal to resume the winding journey to the Rindu Alam Restoran near the summit of the Puncak Pass, a 1,500-metre mountain pass connecting Bogor to Bandung. "Rindu means homesick," Daniel said. "Alam means nature, monsieur." Daniel was studying French and had decided that I would be "Monsieur" for the day.

The Homesick for Nature Café was essentially an Indonesian truck stop and traveller's rest. But it was the closest thing we could find to a country tearoom in the area. What it lacked in charm it made up for in the view of the tea gardens below. It was sublime.

We wended our way through the usual crowd of vendors who lurked about the entrance selling mostly bead necklaces, bracelets and other forms of jewelry. There was no sign of the cheap postcards that had been forced on us by young men at the botanical gardens, all desperate to survive the economic crisis of the moment.

Inside the large restaurant, business was booming and the window seats were almost all taken by thirsty Indonesians drinking huge beer mugs full of what turned out to be tea. We managed to find a window table and the menus came promptly. Several items caught my eye and some turned my stomach: fish head, tripe or mutton soup, oxtail satay, beef brain stewed in coconut milk, fresh orange juice with eggs.

Daniel had already starting ordering but I quickly pointed to the gado gado (raw vegetables covered in peanut sauce), ayam gudesh (jackfruit cooked in coconut milk) and the ikan bakar (fried or BBQed fish). "Oui, monsieur," Daniel agreed, noting my distress.

And of course we ordered our beer mugs brimming with the low-grade tea that is served locally. We opted against egg tea and other beverages such as milk and egg, milk and soda, egg and honey, zurzak (sirsak), belimbing (star fruit) or avocado juice.

The whole meal for three came to a pittance (48,000 rupiah or about $10). Tossed in for free was a view of the flat valley below cut into patches by trails that zigzagged through the tea estates. "Magnifique, n'est-ce pas, monsieur?"

Tea workers getting set to dry the fresh-picked leaves
in Java, Indonesia.

Johnny had stayed with the van and was revving the engine as
we worked our way along the gauntlet of vendors. Next stop Cisarua
and the Gunung Mas or Golden Mountain Tea Estate. I secretly
hoped we could escape another encounter with the pluckers.

Tea plantations are peaceful looking places but they are also
commercial enterprises and workplaces. At Gunung Mas, they em-
ploy about 2,000 people. About 90 per cent of the 1,500 pluckers are
women. Another 500 of them work in cinnamon harvesting and production and 300 more produce quinine. I had no idea that quinine
grew on trees.

This I learned from a foreman at the Gunung Mas, while he led
us through the new, faster green tea production process. The tour began up in the rafters of a large building where the withering bins

were being filled with sacks full of leaves that we had seen being plucked a few hours before.

When we had seen all the stages of production, smelled the final product (both the refined exports and the low-quality locals), and turned down a chance to buy some, we thanked our guide and turned to go.

A man at the entrance tried to sell me a painting of the pluckers who had chased me away like a symphony of angry swans. I said no. We were late for our afternoon cuppa at the nearby Taman African Safari where we would sip to the Sumatran tiger's roar and the rare song of the Lesser Bird of Paradise.

3 EUROPE

The tearoom "is a place for the imagination as a temporary refuge for religious feeling. It is a place for emptiness, inasfar as it is almost totally bare, apart from the minimum aesthetic requirements. It is a place of incomplete symmetry, perfect only in the realm of the imagination."

– *The Book of Tea* written by Kakuzo Okakura (1862-1913).

Bodington's sits across the street from the former home
of English poet John Keats and overlooks a Bellini
fountain in Rome.

Many European tearooms seem to epitomize the expression East is East and West is West and never the twain shall meet. In Asian tearooms tea is served with the air of an ancient ceremonial rite of passage, which it probably once was. In European tearooms a much younger set of traditions kicks into place. All sense of honoured ceremony seems to whither and be replaced by the bustle of people in a hurry to get their cuppa and go back to work. Still, there exist some notable exceptions.

Mariage Frères
A high tea in the City of Lights, love and far too much rain

Ah, to be in Paris in the spring time! Notre Dame, the Louvre, the Left Bank, the Latin Quarter. It's all so romantic, so frantic and brash. But what does the City of Lights offer tea lovers, especially on an unseasonably cold day? Why, it's Mariage Frères, as bright a beacon to tea drinkers as the Moulin Rouge is to club goers and Les Galeries Lafayette is to shoppers.

I had taken a brisk stroll that morning, watching Parisians walk their dogs through the Champs de mars under the gaze of the Eiffel Tower, perhaps the grandest urban landmark of them all. Along rue Bosquet and its side streets, butchers had their rotis spinning with freshly killed chickens. A chocolatier pranced around a chocolate 'bouquet'. Fruit vendors polished apples and arranged oranges in detailed symmetrical formations.

I hopped on a No. 80 bus and sat next to an old woman holding her dog in her lap. The tea-cup-sized beast was dressed in leather. In seats nearby men stinking of cigarette smoke, espresso stains on their jackets, silently read *Le Parisien* sports pages and complained about the cool weather.

I disembarked not far from the Champs Elysses, shopping playground of the wealthy, and walked up rue du Faubourg St Honore to No. 260. There, in all its wood-panelled splendour, sat what is possibly the finest tearoom in all of Paris and certainly the oldest, founded in 1854.

In this great city of thousands of *bar-salons, brasseries, boites de nuit* and an endless parade of incomparable cuisine, I had found a tearoom – *un vrai salon de thé* – a perfect little tearoom like no other tearoom in Paris and possibly *le tout Europe.*

Mariage Frères doesn't just look the part; it feels like an actual tearoom. It's not at all like the hyphenated "tea-rooms" spotted in other Paris arrondissements where you will get a bag on a saucer and some hot water with a biscuit or two not much bigger than an aspirin. Mariage Frères is the Betty's of France.

I kept that thought to myself as a reference to the famed Betty`s, possibly Britain`s finest example of a celebrated tearoom, would probably not go down well on the French side of the English Channel. Also, my comparison might be a slight exaggeration. We wouldn`t want Paris to get a bigger swelled head than it already has.

Still, Mariage Frères is the quintessential tearoom no matter where you travel for your tea. Everything about it was perfectly designed, carefully thought out, precisely placed, precision made. In that sense it is the equal of Betty's.

Mariage Frères sits in its tea-traffic-stopping magnificence at a busy street corner where I admired the distinctive wood paneling before passing through the front doors. No neon here. Just the familiar yellow circle logo with too much black lettering: "*Les meilleurs crus. La grande tradition.*" Tea from China, India, Ceylon and Formosa. And the pen and ink drawings of tea plants, pickers' sacks, tea chests and wooden barrels. Ornate, busy, wordy, but this is the symbol of a tearoom of distinction.

Once inside I saw two large samovars – one silver, one bronze – standing between two glass-windowed, floor-to-ceiling cabinets. To the left, deeper into the shop, was an extensive range of teapots. Indeed, everywhere there was a shelf, there was a teapot. I was surrounded by tea paraphernalia with every item labeled "Mariage Frères."

Tea books, a small library of them, sat on shelves beside me as I took a seat at a small table near the window. *La boite a thé* by Gilles Brochard, *La Tasse a Thé – Connaissances et mémoires européens*, a tea novel by Albert Kaempfen, *Le Thé – Livre du connaisseur* by Jane Pettigrew, *Historie du Thé* by Paul Butel.

All around me were large round tea canisters – red, blue, green, yellow, black – and the shop's far walls were lined with black tin boxes of tea from around the world. Teas from China: Five Dynasties, King of Keemun and Oriental Beauty. Teas from India: Darjeelings from Margaret's Hope estates, Assam's from Napuk, Nunsuch from Nilgiri and Lover's Leap from Sri Lanka. Teas from Thailand: Thai Beauty, Opium Hill and Siam Club. Teas from Vietnam, Russia, Persia, Turkey, Australia, Brazil, Kenya, Uganda and Rwanda.

Among the signature teas exported around the world by Mariage Frères was the distinctive tasting Marco Polo Rouge from South Africa. And the list of superb brews goes on and on. As founder Henri Mariage put it long ago, "a perfume of adventure and of poetry invades each cup of tea." Thus there will be no smoking in his tearoom because the smell of tobacco "doesn't go well with the smell of *nos thés.*"

And then there was the food, the delicacies of the Mariage Frères oven and kitchen. For Mariage Frères, this is known as tea gastronomy where they produce a "mélange of the noblest of tea flavours" with their meals, their patisseries and confiseries in order to "poetically ravage the palate of connoisseurs."

Lunch could be *langoustines au thé vert, salades* with dressing made with Lapsang Souchong, smoked salmon with Tencho Uji tea from Japan, or "Snob Salad" with the flavour of Matcha tea, also Japanese. But taking tea at this posh venue doesn't come cheap.

Prices range from $20-25 for afternoon tea. Brunch is known as *Le Classique*, a mixture of salad, seafood and fresh baked pastries from the Patisserie du Chariot colonial. Cost: $30 plus your tea at $10 and up. One can also order a "mosaic of sandwiches," surrounding a *"Croque monsieur MF"* with smoked salmon, at $35.

Tea cocktails anyone? Yes, you can indulge in Lassi de Mandalay (fermented milk with a drop of Mandalay tea sirop). The Mousse de Jade is cold milk frothed with Matcha green tea. Or try the Fleuve Eternel, tea Nil Rouge with a mix of freshly squeezed orange and grapefruit juices.

Even the jams and jellies are made with tea. "It is a secret what is inside the jar," said my soft-spoken waiter, Emmanuel. I guessed at the ingredients but was far off the mark. What tasted like crabapple with nutmeg was made from oranges, pineapples and mangoes. It was exotically and mysteriously called Pharoum. Another, made of vanilla and cannelle, was named Bourbon.

As tea is served, plates rattle oh so delicately and are quickly muffled by the gloved hands of a caring server. Even the clatter of the "lunch tea" crowd is subdued by the high ceilings and the tendency to whisper within the inner sanctum of tea dining.

Mariage Frères is not far from the Arc de Triomphe area with its hubbub of shoppers and teenagers slinging their mobile phones from ear to ear. But here inside Mariage Frères one hears only the muted murmurs of diners, the quiet request for an order of some carefully prepared tart or loaf, the silent wave of a hand for *l'addition SVP* at the end of a fine culinary experience.

Waiters dressed in long white aprons or beige cotton suits rush about seating guests upstairs and down. A muslin sac is used to prepare perfect cups of Marco Polo, Maharajah and Gengis Khan tea, just some of *les mélanges classiques*. Other waiters are sprucing up the tiers of baked goods.

A dour young man in rumpled beige sits in the money cage at centre shop. He could be a model for one of Charles Dickens's accountants. There he sits dutifully counting francs as ladies dressed in expensive casuals from one of Paris's 'grands surfaces' (shopping centres) pass him their plastic.

Downstairs, a well-dressed older couple enjoys a lunch of *saumon fume de Norvege* and *terrine de foie gras de canard maison*. Newlyweds sit quietly, doting on each other and nibbling at *fleurs de courgettes farcie* and *melee de salade d'herbes aux radis noirs*.

Nearby is a tiny tea museum with its modest teapot collection, several *tasses a moutaches*, the quaint teacups made for men with moustaches, some antique tea measuring spoons, a wood and metal canister, tea chests that once transported bulk teas from far off lands, tea scales, more samovars and tea caddies.

Who knows what clandestine affairs these walls have witnessed? Could it be that the latest sex *scandale* had its origins here among the cacophony of whispered *commandes*? What intrigues are planned to the tinkle of teacups on saucers, the soft ruffle of starched linen napkins, the sharp ring of Sheffield silver on white china?

Mariage Frères describes what they do as the "*Art Francais du Thé.*" This art "embraces the spirit of the beverage, resulting in sage combinations of the cultural, aesthetic and gustative." It is in a "spirit of elegance and simplicity" that Mariage Frères evokes "a sense of far-off journeys and legends inspired by the vast universe of tea."

It may be the flowery language of an earlier century, but there is nothing quite so satisfying on a cold spring afternoon in Paris as taking a cup of fine imported tea at Mariage Frères. Indeed, there are few tearooms that serve tea with as much panache and passion as does this grand old tearoom in the heart of the French capital.

Ode to a Roman Tearoom
Taking tea in the Eternal City with the ghost of John Keats

When the great English poet John Keats succumbed to tuberculosis in 1821, there was no Babington's English Tearooms to be seen from his bedroom window on the other side of the Spanish Steps in Piazza di Spagna, the famed English enclave in the heart of the Eternal City of Rome.

It would take another seventy-two years before a pair of enterprising women founded the exclusive tearooms. But had Babington's been next door to the beloved Keats, he surely would have written a poem about it even if he could not afford to take afternoon tea there back then…or now.

He also might have discussed politics with tearoom co-founder Anna Maria Babington whose ancestry included Thomas Babington Macauley, the nineteenth-century historian. Religion also might have been an apt topic in tea-table conversation with her New Zealand-born collaborator, Isabel Cargill. Her ancestor, Donald Cargill, a staunch Calvinist, died for accusing Charles II of "treason, tyranny and lechery," or so says the book published to celebrate Babington's one-hundredth anniversary in 1993.

Looking down from Keats's bedroom window, one sees the bustle of the piazza on a chilly January afternoon. The pigeons wonder why their perch on the Column of the Immaculate Conception is so cold. In a few days, Rome will see snow for the first time in four years. St. Peter's Basilica, home to popes the centuries over, will be momentarily dotted with great flakes, creating a white carpet before its giant, half-dismantled nativity scene.

Despite the weather, lovers stroll arm in arm up the steps to the old French, not Spanish, Church of the Trinita dei Monti. There are the teenagers sitting in rows, chirping at each other like the tiny nightingale that Keats praised in an ode that every English-speaking school child remembers having to memorize.

There is the famous fountain, sculpted by Bernini and son, where even in winter the crowds gather round the bow and stern of its centerpiece, an ancient sailing vessel that might have carried a Grecian urn or two in its day. Not far off is Trevi Fountain where tourists stomp impatiently in an effort to have their photographs taken and then toss their yen, pennies and centimes over their shoulders to ensure their return to Rome.

To the right, as you stare up the steps and say a polite but firm "No" to the persistent rose seller, there is Babington's with its sign etched in stone as if to announce its permanent status in the city of Caesars.

Outside, Asians and Romanians sell trinket-sized cars and trucks that they are operating noisily by remote control. Odd versions of the Pied Piper. The children are fascinated, but the parents are searching for safety. They want an escape from the non-stop thoroughfare of saints and sinners, suckers and out-of-luckers, lovers and strangers from all over the world who come to Rome to pray at its cathedrals, marvel at its antiquities, enfold themselves in its art, and on occasion to drink tea.

Babington's, sitting unobtrusively nearby, is that refuge. But you have to look for its entrance – and you have to be prepared to pay the high price for the honour of taking tea there. It will cost you an exorbitant nine euros (about $16) to warm your insides with a cup of Babington's "Special Blend," a mixture of Ceylon, Darjeeling and China teas. The "Royal Blend" will cost you E9.50. It's made from "China Keemun, Darjeeling Quality Leaf and Formosa Fancy Oolong donated to H.M. Queen Elizabeth during her visit to Rome."

The cheapest tea on the menu, with the familiar Babington's black cat logo perched on its cover as it is on virtually everything in the tearoom, is E8 for "Pinhead Gunpowder." It's described as a tea "rolled into balls" with a "pungent taste."

The most expensive tea is "Yin Zhen" or "Silver Needles" described as "white tea produced by the "imperial plucking" method performed at dawn on only two days a year." The special privilege will cost you from E20 up to a mind-numbing $35 a cup.

The top scented tea, "Jasmine Dragon Phoenix Pearl," lags far behind at E18.50. That's also the price tag for indulging in "Gyokuro Organic" used in the Japanese tea ceremony. The price drops to a low of E7.50 if you choose one of the tisanes, including Rooibos, Lemon Verbena and Mate, the popular South American brew.

From across the street, poverty-ridden poets may stare down from the wonderful book-lined rooms of the Keats-Shelley Memorial House founded in 1909, but they don't dare enter the tearooms across the way. They would be broke in less than half a cuppa. Besides, *vino della casa* would be cheaper by far and would perhaps more readily assist them in seeking out their muses.

If, perchance, some British poets urged their publishers to send an advance on a future book of rhymes, they would be able to sit in an atmosphere that reminds them of home. At Babington's they would sit on the dark wood benches and chairs, their writing implements stored safely on the shelf found under each table. They would enjoy the quiet of the black and white rooms, bouncing from antique wall clock to leaded windows decorated with white lace under burgundy drapes.

A young server would ask in Italian-accented English, "What would you like today?" Said poets would look at the star-shaped lighting that hangs from the high ceiling or gaze upon the wall lighting, an arrangement of three white flowers, Christmas cactus perhaps, with its cascading green metal leaves. They might lean over to smell the freshly cut yellow, white and red daisies on the table.

Like all poets, you are hungry. You drool over the thought of taking Babington's Special High Tea. How deliciously tempting: *Piccoli tramezzini misti* (assorted sandwiches), Crumpets *caldi con sciroppo d'acero* (maple syrup) and *pasticceria mignon* ("little cakes"). How absolutely out of the question at E24.

A plate of scones would set you back E11; English muffins, E8.50; toast, E5 (E8 if it's cinnamon or "*toast con canella*" and E10 if it's French). You are tempted to pocket some of the Sheffield silver and hawk it later to cover the cost. The teapots, by Arthur Price of England, are too bulky to smuggle undetected. You would never make it past airport security.

If you're an American poet and flush from your latest book sale, you could sample one of Babington's famous hamburgers. Yes, the fancy tearoom introduced such fare after the First World War when a friend advised them of its lucrative popularity. Fast food in a traditional tearoom? Yes, but don't expect Macdonald's prices. These burgers will run you as high as E24 for the "*Negrino*" (on rice with cream cheese sauce). A club sandwich is also offered (E17.50 to E19).

If you're a British poet, shepherd's pie, Welsh rarebit, "blushing bunny" (toast with mushrooms, tomatoes and cheese sauce) or a ploughman's lunch are also available. Regrettably they, too, come at prices you won't be able to afford unless you have just won a coveted poetry prize or scored a writer's grant from some rich benefactor.

On your way back to the Spanish Steps and the resumed craziness of a Roman holiday, the street activity has intensified. The shops have re-opened at 3 p.m. after the daily ritual of the Italian siesta. You will see postcard and souvenir sellers, all offering the same clay replicas of the Colosseum, the Forum, the Pantheon, Piazza di Venezia and the Sistine Chapel.

The crowds will rush into leather and lingerie stores (the January sales mean price cuts of 20-50 per cent) and they will be confronted by an aggressive sales clerk. Food shops will have tarted up their windows with hanging prosciutto hams, colourfully packaged Tuscan paneforte and tri-coloured pasta.

You will need to go to an Autobanco for more cash. Your last seven euros have gone to buy a small yellow tin of loose tea. It contains only an ounce but you also will get the black cat logo that is imprinted on it as a souvenir. Babington's store is full of other memorabilia, too, including the outrageously expensive metal creamers and sugar bowls with the black cat soldered to the lid.

Would Keats have written an ode to that cat and to all the other cats that roam the great city teeming around Piazza di Spagna and beyond? No doubt he would have. Had he lived long enough to enjoy such a fanciful tea, perhaps he might even have been inspired to write *The Party of Lovers* here:

> Pensive they sit, and roll their languid eyes,
> Nibble their toast, and cool their tea with sighs,
> Or else forget the purpose of the night,
> Forget their tea – forget their appetite.

Then again, perhaps he would have penned an ode especially to celebrate this great English tearoom in the heart of Rome. He probably could not have afforded to do anything else.

Betty's of Harrogate
Tearoom champion of all England

Tearooms are almost as common in the United Kingdom as McDonald's are in North America, but that's where the comparison ends. McDonald's prides itself on serving good old American hamburgers and that makes some Americans feel like they've never left home. The classic British tearoom, on the other hand, is usually quiet, quaint and ever so British.

Whichever end of the country you travel to, from East Anglia to Gretna Green to Land's End to the Isle of Wight, you will find a tearoom ready to serve you a steaming hot cup of your favourite Orange Pekoe.

Tearooms are so plentiful in Britain that some towns are in danger of losing essential shops just to make room for another one. They're everywhere from Portsmouth in the south to Inverness in the north. The smallest hamlet has its own tearoom, possibly two. They are even more ubiquitous than that most ubiquitous of things, the British pub.

The Yorkshire Dales are no exception to this fact of English life. Indeed Yorkshire is home to the champion, the Queen, the *sine qua non* of British tearooms, Betty's of Harrogate. But don't take my word for it. The British Tea Council judged Betty's to be the 1994 "Top tea place of the year."

"For the past seventy-five years, locals and tourists alike have been willing to travel long distances and even queue to enjoy a cup of Betty's perfectly brewed tea," says a council's news release. It adds that the Harrogate shop "snatched the title from its namesake in Ilkey," a short jaunt from the famed Bronte parsonage in Haworth where the beloved Bronte sisters lived and wrote their popular period novels. Then there's Betty's in North Allerton and Betty's in York. Must not forget Taylors, a Betty's partner, also in York.

Whoa! Can tea really be this good? Well, for starters, they offer thirty-five different teas. Then there's the food tray displaying several famous Yorkshire specialities. And there's a gorgeous mix of British and Swiss-style pastries.

Whoa! Can tea really be this good? Well, for starters, they offer 35 different teas. Then there's the food tray displaying several famous Yorkshire specialties. And there's a gorgeous mix of British and Swiss-style pastries.

It's not cheap, of course. A pot of, say, Special Estate Darjeeling or Tippy Assam will run you $4.50 and that's just tea for one. A Yorkshire "Fat Rascal," described by the *Radio Times* in a glowing tribute to Betty's as "a smiling fruity scone with cherry eyes and almond teeth," costs almost $5. A "Traditional Yorkshire Afternoon Tea," with another specialty, "Yorkshire curd tart," is about $18.

Still, a trip to Betty's is as essential to one's visit to this sheep-in-the-meadows section of the British landscape, with its luscious dales and its craggy moors, as Yorkshire pudding is to a roast beef dinner.

This is James Herriot country and the author of *All Creatures Great and Small* must surely have made numerous visits to a Betty's near him. It's also where they film one of my favourite British television shows, *Heartbeat.* Tea, though not often at a Betty's, plays its part in the endless crime-solving that takes place each week in an unlikely Yorkshire village.

When you tire of adoring the stunning landscape that provides the backdrop for Heartbeat, make a stop at the Royal Baths. They're what made Harrogate famous in the Victorian era and those decadent times still seep from every side street even today. Enjoy an early morning cuppa before settling into a leisurely Turkish steam. Emerge somewhat lighter and well prepared for another trip to Betty's to indulge. Your waistline be damned!

Have cream tea (about $8) after you've walked the 200-acre Stray, a huge inner-city park, or the beautifully manicured Valley Gardens with their endless flowerbeds and duck ponds. Then take high tea while you discuss whether Dame Agatha Christie really was hiding at the nearby Old Swan Hotel. Her disappearance for ten days in 1926 led to what was dubbed the greatest "man hunt" in British history.

Had Dame Agatha taken a break from writing one of her who-done-its and ventured from her secret hideaway, she might have gone directly to Betty's for tea. The Queen of Crime would have felt right at home seeing her tea brought on an elegant silver tea service by a woman dressed in a black and white maid's uniform. Would she have had to gloat a while as she waited in the long line of customers anxious to make Betty's even richer? Decidedly not.

Betty's was a mere seven years old, when Dame Agatha seques-tered herself at the Swan. A childless Swiss confectioner started it in 1919. Over the intervening years, Betty's has become a multi-million-dollar business run by the founder's nephew, Victor Wild. He thinks Betty's was named after a little girl in the family, but no one knows for sure.

"Not your usual scone-baker," as the *Radio Times* puts it, Wild still has employees do some training in Switzerland. If one wanted to start a tearoom, this is where one would be advised to come to learn how to do it successfully. Betty's is a post-graduate-level tearoom.

Oh, and lest you think that all this talk of tea is a bit trite, no less a voice than the Old Thunderer itself, the *Times of London*, would beg to differ. On July 24, 1994, it ran a front-page story entitled "Six cuppas a day keep cancer away."

Is that why Betty's is so popular? Is it that *the* quality tearoom of the north country is offering immunization from the dreaded dis-ease if not an outright cure? Possibly, but the more likely attraction is the thought of crunching into their Yorkshire fat rascals. That and the sheer pleasure of knowing you won't be disappointed when you finally get seated at Betty's table.

Cornish Delight
Farm cream tea in England's Deep South

I experienced my first taste of farm cream tea at Trethorne Farm near Launceston at the Cornwall-Devon border. I also got a first-class education on Cornwall's thriving dairy industry from Winston and Dorothy Davey, the proprietors. They provided some quirky on-the-job explanations of how milk products are made.

I especially enjoyed seeing how clotted cream comes from boiling down raw milk until it is as thick as butter and almost as yellow. It's not a table cream or a double cream – the British name for thick whipped cream – but a "proper" cream meant to be spooned out in generous dollops. In a way, it's an excellent, though even more fattening, substitute for butter.

Trethorne also had its own tearoom where Dorothy's home-made scones and strawberry jam were born to be smothered in the rich cream produced daily at the creamery. This gave me a high-quality comparison for future tastings as I rambled through the tiny hedge-rowed highways that turn the rolling Cornish countryside into a checkerboard of farmlands.

Determined to discover the finest cream teas in the region, I roamed far from my Trethorne base. I spent many an afternoon ooing and ahhing as I indulged in a parade of traditional cream teas: two scones, jam (usually strawberry, although Cornwall is renowned for berries of many kinds), a sinfully large serving of thick clotted cream and a pot of steaming dark tea.

Butter was rarely served and the tea almost always came in a metal pot – a no-no for real tea drinkers who prefer ceramic or porcelain pots – and a smaller side pot of hot water. The price ranged from about $2.50 to $5, cheap for late lunch in a Britain where the cost of living easily matches Canada's.

My British tea travels also taught me that Cornish cream teas are traditionally served with two white-flour scones; they're rarely baked with currants or cheese. But at the risk of dangerously expanding my already sizeable girth, I discovered that the finest of all cream teas offer "Cornish splits" as well as scones.

Splits are delicious fine-white-flour rolls that are ripped in half and covered in clotted cream and jam. Children often squeal with delight when offered a "thunder and lightning," a split doused in treacle and topped with cream. Or is it the other way round?

As I roamed the Cornish tea trail, I was delighted by many unique tearooms. Those along the Cornish Riviera, especially at Polperro, were appealing for their view of the inner harbour. Then there was the secluded tearoom near Gweek set up on the Lord of the Rings theme from the J.R.R. Tolkein fantasy. (Tolkein apparently crafted his imaginary land from memories of Cornwall.)

Further down the east coast is the gorgeous Helford River area, the setting for Daphne Du Maurier's *Frenchman's Creek* and the birthplace of her *Jamaica Inn* heroine. From the tearoom, I could see palm trees swaying. Still further along the peninsula are the story-book villages of Coverack and Cadgwith where fresh crab sand-wiches join tea and scones on the lunch menu.

Moving west, I enjoyed wonderful cream teas at tearooms that rivaled those anywhere in Britain for quaintness. One even served gooseberry pie and all had that special treat that other tearooms lacked: rich clotted cream fresh from nearby dairy farms. As I trav-elled further up the west coast I stopped for tea at cute Boscastle, at Tintagel (where the legendary knights of the Round Table took tea) and even as far north as picturesque Clovelly in Devon.

Truth be told, my search uncovered more mediocre cream teas than great ones. Regrettably the tea was often served in those guar-anteed-to-spill metal pots and it was almost always a run-of-the-mill brand. Rarely did I get a top-quality tea like my favourite Assam, Darjeeling or Ceylon.

Specialty blends such as Earl Grey or Lady Grey were more likely to be served. The jam was usually strawberry, although I did get apricot, blackcurrant or even hedgerow jam from berries picked from the never-ending Cornish hedgerows. But even the most hum-ble of tearooms was far more satisfying than any outing to a McDonald's.

My best cream tea experience was at the Mariner's Lodge in Porthcurno in southeast Cornwall near Land's End. It was also the most expensive at almost $5. It was worth every penny farthing for each morsel was as delectable as the magnificent view. There I watched children swim in the chilly azure blue English Channel, while enjoying a visit to the world-famous Minack outdoor theatre where applause for Shakespeare's tragedies and comedies shakes the rocky cliffs of the surrounding countryside.

Still, on my return to Trethorne I had to admit that there was something extra-special about Dorothy Davey's farm tearoom. Clotted cream is never so good as when it's fresh and there is nothing quite like tasting scones that I watched being baked. Needless to say, I'm still trying to lose the ten pounds I gained while pursuing such rigorous and demanding tea research.

Tea Along the Bosphorus
Turkey lubricates its carpet-selling economy with offerings of tea all day long

From the muezzin's first eerie-sounding prayers echoing through the narrow streets around the Blue Mosque at sunrise each morning, Istanbul wakes up with coffee on its mind. Yet tea is what makes old Stamboul's economy rumble along all day long.

Tea is the city's ancient custom and its constant pastime, with hundreds of tea gardens (*cay bachesi*) satisfying a near unquenchable thirst for the black liquid that is at the heart of Istanbul's cultural, business and social life.

Turkish tea, which is grown near Rize on the Black Sea, is black but that's where similarities to other teas ends. This tea is double-boiled until a spoon could almost stand up in it. It is such a presence in everyday life here that it is hard to imagine the city's commerce functioning without it.

Tea, dark, strong, deliciously sweet Turkish tea, is what greases the local business machinery and keeps it whirring frantically in the covered bazaars, the food-laden *lokantas* and a thousand carpet-sellers' dens in the throbbing heart of this mysterious gateway to both Europe and Asia.

Apple tea, kiwifruit tea, sage tea, hibiscus tea and others are found everywhere in Byzantium, as the city was known in Byzantine times. Then it was Constantinople and only after the modernization ushered in by Mustafa Kemal Ataturk in the 1920s, ending the Ottoman Empire and the rule of the sultans, did it become Istanbul.

Even Ataturk's mausoleum in Ankara, the capital, has on display the tea ware of state, gifts from the Shah of Iran and a dozen other potentates who visited the modern leader who transformed his country from developing backwater to modern European trading nation.

Tugging at the easternmost corner of Europe and then linked to Asia by sprawling high metal bridges, Istanbul draws its many charms from both east and west.

It is a belly dancer beckoning the traveller to venture within to gaze upon the treasures of the sultans housed at the opulent Topkapi, Dolmabahce or Ciragan palaces. But it is also a modern wizard all wired up and cellphone-equipped for business. Its five-star hotels glisten high above Taksim Square across the Golden Horn near Galata Tower.

Walk through the age-old cisterns that once brought water to the city. Get your muscles pounded at a Turkish bath (hamam). Eat *al fresco* at your choice of fifty seafood restaurants at Kumpkapi, once an old fishing village. Buy a simit (a cross between a bagel and a pretzel) piping hot from a street vendor who carries a hundred of them piled high on a platter that sits atop his head. Or pick up the catch of the day from a bobbing fishing boat cum floating kitchen. And always there is tea.

Everywhere men rush among the crowd swinging brass trays loaded with tiny, tulip-shaped glasses of dark brown Turkish tea. They are on their way to a carpet-seller's tent or a ceramics shop in the Grand Bazaar, the largest covered market in Europe. They run through the Egyptian (a.k.a. Spice) Bazaar stopping at the jewellery shops crammed beside sweets counters where Turkish Delight is stacked high and pistachios dribble from huge cloth sacks.

The custom is to offer tea without obligation to buy. There is, however, an obligation to listen to the sales pitch and it can be incredibly detailed. Carpets are as ubiquitous as tea in Turkey and you will sooner or later be compelled to sit through a lecture on the intricacies of carpet weaving. The tea – usually requiring sugar to appeal to the western palate – makes the oncoming spiel more tolerable. But beware! It can also induce you to begin bargaining for a carpet you never wanted in the first place.

When I asked about the little girls sitting erect on stools as they gazed into their looms, the seller quickly assured me that they live better and are better schooled with him than they would be at home. Still, watching the tiny fingers weave the most delicate patterns fostered guilty feelings about child labourers. Perhaps the carpet man thought another glass of tea would wash away the guilt?

***

If you travel by ferry, either up the Bosphorus or perhaps to Princes Islands in the Sea of Maramara, you will constantly be irritated by the nasal bark of a waiter. "Cay! Cay!" you will hear him yell the Turkish word for tea as he carries his tray through the crowds of long-trousered Turks and short-panted tourists looking for a place to cool off.

Awash in this sea of Turkish tea, it seemed unlikely that we would find a unique western tearoom. Oh, there is the old Pera Pelas hotel. That's where Agatha Christie wrote *Murder on the Orient Express* or so local legend has it. It has a cafe that offers afternoon tea but the service is unsophisticated, the pastries ordinary, and the atmosphere has gone beyond faded elegance to jaded has-been.

The love seats and awning-roofed chairs are quaint but uncomfortable and the cost of a cup of bagged tea was 300,000 Turkish lira (about $4 US). It's a treat to see the old-fashioned metal-framed elevator and the dark wood-panelled rooms where Dame Agatha scratched out her famous plot. But as a tearoom, the Pera Pelas is long past its prime. If she were alive today, it's highly doubtful that Dame Agatha would be caught dead taking tea here.

That disappointment behind me, I journeyed along the European shore of the Bosphorus until I found what I was seeking. Fortunately, taxis are cheap in Istanbul and the route, for better or worse, is a bit like driving along the Riviera.

A stop in the village of Ortakoy revealed how young Turks spend their weekends. Near the old mosque at the foot of the Bosphorus Bridge leading to Asia, they could be seen dining on potato skins, fried fish, wonderfully thick yoghurt with honey and gallons of tea sipped at an outdoor bar while playing backgammon.

Further on near the Mehmet Fatih Bridge, the second magnificent crossing into Asia, I came to Rumeli Hisar. A well-preserved castle sits high above the water there and below it young men dove into the body of water that Lord Byron made famous in the West through his poetry and reported daring. Later I would see whole families barbecuing fish caught with long poles earlier in the day.

Turning from the sea, I spotted a sign that read Edwards of Hisar, an exclusive men's clothing store. I had no need for a new suit, but just above it, marked only by a hanging bronze tea kettle and a sign that simply said "tearoom," was the object of my search.

A few steps and I entered a time warp. Here in the outer heart of this Turkish metropolis was a perfect little English tearoom elaborately decorated down to the last detail. Vintage tea canisters, ceramic animals, and paintings of teapots adorned the walls at the entrance.

At the doorway to the second room sat an odd-shaped display table each tier of which held a plastic model of a full English breakfast as well as scones and fruit tarts. A sizable teapot collection covered the far wall of the large centre room. At one end of a Turkish carpet runner, an armoire housed a selection of Wilson's teas. Six tables were neatly covered in Laura Ashley-style floral cloth.

Entering the third room was like walking into something out of the British Raj in India. A giant tiger-skin rug and a mammoth set of buffalo antlers first caught my eye. A more studied glance spied some antique golf clubs, a pair of polished riding boots, some clay elephants, an aging rugby ball and two silver tea services on a wheeled caddy. But wait! As I turned to leave the room, I saw a taxidermist's glass encasement containing two new-born tigers, just two days old at the time.

My tour complete, I ordered Imperial China which came in a cheesecloth-like bag from Dammann's of France. It was full-flavoured despite being bagged. The scones, served with honey, were made with whole grain flour and stuffed with sultanas. A cherry juice, offered all over Istanbul by young men in fezes carrying large metal bottles of it on their backs, was tasty without being too sweet. The cost of a full afternoon tea is 1.5 million Turkish lira. Tea alone is 300,000. It sounded unaffordable but amounted to only a few dollars.

Sadly, the service was flawed by the lack of butter, cream or milk. But this was understandable since the Turks never take milk or cream in their tea. It is also quite forgivable when you consider that this tearoom is a singular oasis perched along the Bosphorus amidst the minarets, the wedding-cake palaces and the untold marvels of old Byzantium.

Indeed, it is a small cultural wonder in a city where tea-drinking is as much a part of everyday life as it is further east along the Silk Road toward the birthplace of tea itself, China.

Swiss "Tea-Rooms"
Frustrated in the tea-neutral land of clocks and chocolate

Wodey-Suchard is a tea-room with a hyphen. It didn't start out as a tearoom, and the "Tea-room" sign outside hangs over a window full of chocolate candy. The inlaid hand-lettering below it cast even more doubt on its authenticity. It said "Patisserie-Confiserie-Chocolaterie."

But despite my lingering doubts, as I stepped inside, I saw that it was indeed a tearoom situated within the quiet downtown streets of Neuchatel, a picturesque old city in the northwest corner of Switzerland.

Then owner, Christian Cuche, born in Neuchatel, was in his thirties when we met. He and his wife Vanessa bought the store, the oldest in a city dripping with chocolate lore. It was here in 1825 that Philippe Suchard began his climb to world fame for brands names like Milka and Toblerone. But it wasn't Suchard who made the business grow. He was a good chocolatier, as Cuche put it, but his brother-in-law, a "Monsieur Wodey," was the business head.

The Cuches were simple chocolate makers who seized the opportunity to be part of the legend. Wodey and Suchard had several factories in the region, one at nearby Serrieres, and many Neuchatelois were touched by the Suchard family and fortunes. There was even a local archive dedicated to their family history. The empire, later taken over by Kraft, extended to Lorrach and Bludenz in Germany with sales centres in Paris, London and New York.

While waiting for my tea, I noted a small, framed sign on each linen-covered table. It said hot chocolate was the house specialty and explained that, "I mix different sorts of chocolate to try to rediscover the hot cocoa my grandmother made for me."

Still, Wodey-Suchard was as good a tearoom as I would find in Neuchatel and possibly all of Switzerland, for I had trouble finding its equal even in old-town Geneva. Don't get me wrong. There are "tea-rooms" everywhere in this politically neutral, multilingual, geographical spec of gorgeous lakes and tall mountains, of clocks and chocolate, smack dab in the middle of Europe.

Indeed, there are at least three little café-restaurants with signs hastily hung from ornate hooks suggesting that they double or even triple as "tea-rooms." But it is a false front probably designed to attract the British traveler always anxious to imbibe in their national hot beverage.

"Tea-room has a foreign sound," explained Cuche. "Anything foreign also attracts the locals. It's like having a French chef in an American restaurant. It doesn't matter how good he is, the locals will still be curious."

Of course, most Brits will be disappointed with most Swiss tea-rooms, I'm afraid. But it isn't such a huge disappointment at Wodey-

Suchard. There you will find a small but sophisticated selection of teas. Pure Ceylon High Grown is on the menu described as *"une mélange extra-fin et particulierement soigne des Hautes-Plateaux du Sri Lanka."* The menu adds that *"Ce thé de Ceylon est un must,"* revealing that Franglais was unavoidable even here.

"Finest Darjeeling Tea" was described as a *"un mélange des massifs montagneux se situant sur les contreforts de l'Himilaya."* The menu added that *"Ces grandes plantes de Darjeeling donnent la fameuse 'muscate flavour' au thé."* English tea travellers would be most impressed with the bilingualism of the Wodey-Suchard menu.

"Finest Earl Grey Tea," "China Green Tea (thé vert)" and "Thé Wodey" are joined by various tisanes and some flavoured teas. It all sounds quite perfect until the tea itself arrives on a busy May Day holiday.

I'm sad to report that major disappointment awaits the tea lover here. Hot water sits in a Villeroy & Boch cup and saucer on a small fake wooden tray. A second smaller saucer covers the hot water and holds a tea bag. Yes, a bag! It is marked "Goldcastle Tea and Coffee."

Further disappointment arrived with two of the tiniest *"petits fours"* I have ever eaten. There they sat, winking up at me from a small square dish. I've seen pills bigger than these fancy *biscuits*. They were accompanied by three sugar lumps, two white and one brown. Beside these was a chocolate thimble containing cream. The thimble is the most unique aspect of a tea that is a far cry from meeting high British tearoom standards...proper tearooms *sans trait d'union*, that is!

The Wodey-Suchard décor was tearoomish to be sure. Spring flowers pushed their colourful heads out of long planters. But again, disappointment struck when a touch reveals that they are made of plastic and fabric.

A framed poster or two hung from one wall, bragging about the famous "Chocolat Suchard." Some jewelry was framed and mounted on another. A dozen metal chocolate moulds – rabbits and roosters – were perched above the tea bar.

A nameless clock with a white face two feet in diameter hung from a far wall above the large round-arched windows. In a country built on clocks and banks, it was an appropriate addition to the atmosphere.

Amazingly, the tea was good. But the Swiss can only pretend to be true tea drinkers. Coffee is their greater passion. And had I not been spoiled years ago by the *grands cafes crèmes* of Normandy, the watery and muddy Swiss coffee might have appealed.

With tea and coffee a dead bust, I turned to chocolate. I learned that the Cuches worked for more than a year with a local jeweller to perfect a new line of chocolate called "Ensemble" with a humanitarian touch.

As I was leaving, I saw a flat box filled with dark chocolate shapes that could have been mistaken for miniature human bodies. At the centre was a lone white chocolate 'body' linking with the dark bodies. "It was a merger of the art of *confiserie* and the art of *bijouterie*...of food and art," Cuche said.

He didn't pretend that what he did was art in the same vein as the Grand Masters of European painting. "It is down the ladder a ways to be sure," he said. "But it makes my life more interesting to take a plate of fruit and turn it into something attractive, something creatively exciting. Otherwise, the life of a *confisier* would be pretty dull."

***

Not far down the street from Wodey-Suchard sat Schmid tearoom with its breads and rolls and outdoor tables. It was inviting but it was too cool to dine el fresco that day. The Neuchatelois were regularly heard to complain that the rain had hardly ceased since October.

And there is *Bach et Buck*, the *creperie* tearoom on *rue du Premier mai*, the town's main street. It offers one black tea on its menu, a Ceylon, and the rest are tisanes and flavoured teas, a full laminated page of them. You also get a tea strainer with your loose tea, something the Cuches should have copied. But then, tea clearly is not a Swiss drink and Switzerland is decidedly not a tea country.

To Russia With (Tea) Love
Channeling the spirit of H.G. Wells in Russia's Venice

By Soviet standards it wasn't much of a parade on Russia's national Flag Day (August 22). No ballistic missiles, no goose-stepping Red Army corporals, no anti-American speeches. In fact, the people that were sipping "Russian Afternoon Tea" with champagne and red caviar in the lobby of the Hotel Astoria in St. Petersburg probably didn't realize that the day was upon us.

Outside, old St. Isaac's Cathedral towered over the square of that name. Down a jagged street near one of the city's many canals, Rodion Romanovich Raskolnikov did the murderous deed for which his creator Fyodor Dostoyevsky made him so famous and so guilt-ridden in *Crime and Punishment.*

Inside, chocolate flowed in rivulets as it was pumped from an ornate silver fountain behind which stood a woman who looked more like a scullery maid in an Anton Chekov short story than a pastry chef. The chocolate was destined for a plate of freshly spooned crepes.

Back outside and glaring straight at me from St. Isaac's Square sat a statue of Czar Nicholas I, proudly posed atop his horse. He might have been leading the charge against a band of revolutionaries called the Decembrists. The rebels made the first attempt at a Russian revolution back in December of 1825 calling on Nicholas to grant modest reforms. Off they went in irons to Peter and Paul Fortress across the Neva River, their uprising ruthlessly put down and those responsible eradicated.

British writer H.G. Wells might have sat at this very table contemplating matters of historic import when he stayed at the Astoria back in 1914. Might he have been pondering what to write about Russia in his *Outline of History?* This country alone could fill more than a few volumes and has done.

Perhaps H.G. was coveting some of the caviar, champagne and pirozhki (meat-filled pastries), the ingredients that turned this from a common or garden variety tea to a true "Russian" tea. He may have penned notes for one of his famous novels here in this grand room.

Three years later in 1917, Vladimir Ilyich Lenin would set up headquarters in the hotel and provide more than a few moments worthy of note for H.G.'s history book. Of course, it wasn't only left-wing revolutionaries and famous authors who took tea at the Astoria.

The hotel claims with pride that Margaret Thatcher, George W. Bush and Tony Blair sipped Assam and Earl Grey from its Imperial Porcelain china. Lesser luminaries like Chuck Norris, Luciano Pavarotti and Jack Nicholson also found themselves staring out at St. Isaac's Square, but they were more likely to have been knocking back vodka in the Kandinsky Lounge down the hall.

If they stepped out for a stroll they might also have seen another statue, this one more famous than Nicholas. In fact, it may well be the most famous of all the statues in St. Petersburg. It's the czar who founded the city in 1703, capturing the land on the Gulf of Finland from the marauding Swedes. It's Peter the Great, *The Bronze Horseman* in Alexander Pushkin's celebrated poem.

A few stragglers from the Flag Day celebrations over at Alexandrovsky Park snooped around the statue. Yet another couple was having wedding photos taken with Peter on his high horse in the background. At the old fortress still more tourists were squeezing the bronze index finger of another statue of Peter, the gesture said to bring good luck.

Just past the baby orchids on my table (H.G.'s and mine), their lavender petals touched by northern sunshine, I could see the glass cabinets glistening with high-priced amber jewellery akin to what was to be found in the St Petersburg palace of Catherine the Great. By contrast, across the square outside, trinket vendors sporting the usual Russian fur hats, scarves, pens, pins, and ubiquitous matryoshka dolls, were trying to wrench a few roubles from passing tourists.

Cigarette lighters imprinted with the old Soviet hammer and sickle, symbol of communism, were prominently displayed. It seemed an anachronism now since former president and then prime minister Vladimir Putin inaugurated Flag Day to celebrate the new capitalist Russia.

High up on the St. Isaac's colonnade, others who clearly had forgotten to observe the day had paid the one hundred and seventy roubles (about $7) to climb to the top for a peek at the costumed flag wavers far below.

The day's parade had begun near Cafe Singer across the street from imposing Kazan Cathedral. The largest bookstore in St. Petersburg is housed in the unmistakable Singer Sewing Machine Company building on busy Nevsky Prospekt.

About fifty people mostly dressed and painted in white marched in ragtag fashion behind six young female drummers. Here and there a red, white and blue flag appeared. A beauty queen wore a paper sailing ship on her head painted in those same colours.

Along the old capital's most famous street they went with traffic cops clearing the way as two clowns on giant tricycles weaved around them adding to the merriment. It was more like a small-town homecoming than a parade to celebrate the Russian Federation, arguably still the second most powerful country in the world even with all its problems.

At the historic Admiralty spire a few blocks away from the Winter Palace, the one the revolutionaries stormed in 1917, baton twirlers joined the drum majorettes. Art has, of course, replaced revolution in the palace. As part of L'Hermitage it is stormed daily by tourists paying four hundred roubles (about $20) to gawk at some
of the world's great treasures, including some Impressionist masterpieces once stolen by the Nazis, which are now housed therein.

In the Astoria lobby, next to a painting of St. Petersburg's most famous landmark, the Church of Spilled Blood, a fresh copy of the English-language *St. Petersburg Times* reminded readers of Flag Day. An article inside claimed that the Soviet Red Army, not the atomic bomb, ended the Second World War and prime minister Putin warned that bread prices were too high.

Back in the park, Flag Day celebrants heard an opera singer's powerful baritone voice sing of Russia's proud past. Cannon fire boomed spraying red, white and blue confetti among them. And they watched in awe as ballerinas, perhaps from the famed Kirov or Bolshoi ballet companies, wrapped themselves in the colours of their country.

I finished my tea and chocolate-drenched crepe and reminded myself to reread some of St. Petersburg poet Alexander Blok's lyrical love poems or perhaps *The Twelve*, his response to the 1917 revolution.

For now, though, it was time to say farewell to Flag Day and to H.G. Fortified by tea, I was off to chase after Raskolnikov in this storied place of towering literary figures and revolutionaries, this Venice of the North.

Czar Nicholas I oversees St. Isaac's Square in St. Petersburg, Russia, with the Astoria tearoom in the background.

4 NORTH AMERICA

"Tea had come as a deliverer to a land that called for de-liverance; a land of beef and ale, of heavy eating and abundant drunkenness; of gray skies and harsh winds; of strong-nerved, stout-purposed, slow-thinking men and women. Above all, a land of sheltered homes and warm firesides – firesides that were waiting – waiting, for the bubbling kettle and the fragrant breath of tea."

– Agnes Repplier, *To Think of Tea*, 1933.

A tea plucker holds out her harvest in Indonesia.

North America sometimes likes to pose as a tea land, but it really isn't one at all. Whether in Canada, the United States or Mexico, this is primarily a land of coffee drinkers, cafes and coffee houses. It wasn't always so, of course. One need only recall the days before the Boston Tea Party. Perhaps that was the moment in history when tea started to fall out of favour. Since then it's been harder for tea traveler to find our palate's desire. Thanks to the tea gods, however, there are at least a few tearooms worthy of attention and patronage.

The Tea Server Wore Reeboks
Victoria's Empress hotel is Canada's most celebrated tearoom

"What do you mean there are no openings for afternoon tea at the Empress," puffed the man with the Texas drawl. "I came to Victoria expressly to take tea at the Empress Hotel and I'm going to do just that."

You could hardly blame the poor fellow. After all, the grand old Canadian Pacific hotel has been serving a fine afternoon tea since 1908. Everyone has to try it at least once just to say they did. Is it worth the $25 (mid-1990s prices) to relax in the "Tea Lobby" and gaze out at Victoria Harbour.

The Empress is a remnant of British Columbia's colonial past and Victoria is happy to accommodate the old dame by supplying requisite red double-decker tour buses and the stately copper-roofed buildings of the province's Parliament.

Modern ferries ply the waters outside where once sternwheelers did the job. But for the new hotels along the harbourfront and the tiny seaplanes that noisily land and takeoff right in front of the hotel, one could be transported back to that earlier era when tea-drinking was *de rigueur.*

Victoria does uphold the strictest of Victorian tea traditions as did the great British empress Queen Victoria after which the capital of B.C. is named. She took her tea seriously and so does this beautiful coastal city that offers so much to the tea lover, even the most demanding of them and even if they are from Texas.

Alas, the American gentlemen would have to wait his turn. The busy dining reservation agent would hold a seat for him the following day at 2:30 p.m. Then he could personally verify the hotel's claim to be "a beacon to all who hold dear the grandeur and elegance of a simpler time."

Then and only then would he be allowed to taste the fresh home-grown fruit, the home-made raisin scones with Jersey cream and strawberry jam that accompany the Empress's own special blend of tea. And for this demanding fellow the strictly observed dress code, an anomaly in carefree, laidback B.C., would not be a problem.

Years ago, when Empress afternoon tea might cost $13, I made a point of calling from the mainland to confirm that a dress code was in effect. After making the one hour and forty minute ferry crossing from Vancouver's downtown harbour, I was ready for the delicious hot crumpets and honey that were then on the Empress tea menu.

The dress code was clearly marked on a sign at the entrance to the meticulously appointed Tea Lobby, and I had been careful to dress appropriately. So it came as a comical contradiction to notice that the server was wearing a pair of Reeboks while she ladled out the warm honey!

Of course, for those who don't wish to shed their shorts or jogging suits, there are plenty of other tea stops in this city of flowers perched by the sea. In fact, "Victoria has perfected the ritual of afternoon tea," according to a city brochure. "There are dozens of tearooms, from grand and formal to charming and rustic."

On the rustic side, the James Bay Tearoom and Restaurant behind the Parliament Buildings, offers a high tea on Sundays that includes a trifle. The tea is a "Queen's Blend" of Orange Pekoe and Darjeeling from Kraft Canada. And it comes in small Brown Betty covered in a hand-knitted tea cozy. A local lady still mails the tearoom a supply of the cozies even though she has moved to far-off Winnipeg.

The giant blueberry scones are served warm with butter and strawberry jam and they're certainly filling. They are obvious proof that this is a tearoom for tough times, where faded portraits of the Royals adorn every wall and tacky stained-glass lampshades dangle over every table. No match for the opulent Empress.

Authentic would properly describe Murchies a block away from the Empress. The Murchies tea and coffee chain supplies the grand dame with her special "Empress Afternoon" blend, by the way, and they have a reputation to live up to.

In 1894, John Murchie emigrated to B.C. from Scotland where he had learned the art of tea blending. The Canadian-owned company has been importing world-quality teas and winning awards for its blends ever since. Murchie's No. 10 is their signature blend and it's the perfect pick-me-up on a cool coastal morning.

The teashop displays an impressive selection of teas and tea paraphernalia all introduced at the entrance by a quaint old puppet cabinet that depicts three elderly ladies at a tea party. The tearoom offers tea on the sidewalk for much of the year thanks to the mildest climate in an otherwise inclement one throughout most of Canada.

Charmingly noisy might describe the Blethering Place slightly out of the downtown core. Its huge scones are a meal in themselves and the small shop at the entrance offers tea paraphernalia and bulk teas. It's not far from one of the Empress's afternoon tea rivals, the Oak Bay Beach Hotel.

Thankfully quiet describes the tea service offered on the croquet lawn at Point Ellice a short foot-ferry ride from the Empress. The one-hundred-and-eight-year-old Italianate villa served tea to Canada's first prime minister, Sir John A. Macdonald, and to Robert Falcon Scott a.k.a. Scott of Antarctica. You can enjoy high tea there with "the same care and attention to detail Queen Victoria herself came to expect," says a brochure.

Still, there is something special about an Empress tea for the tens of thousands of tourists who annually descend on the city during the summer months. In fact, Victoria has been judged the number one destination of choice in Canada by no less an expert than the *Conde Nast Traveler*. Perhaps that is where our insistent Texan first heard about it.

Like Rudyard Kipling before him, he must have been thoroughly charmed by Victoria's scenic setting. "To realize Victoria you must take all that the eye admires in Bournemouth, Torquay, the Isle of Wight, the Happy Valley at Hong Kong, the Doon, Sorrento, and Camp's Bay," wrote the famous storyteller. "[A]dd reminiscences of the Thousand Islands and arrange the whole around the Bay of Naples with some Himalayas for background."

Also like Kipling, there is little doubt that our tea-drinking Texan would allow himself to be tamed by the Empress. Should he wander into the Empress shop, he might be surprised to find several unique tea items. They might include a translation of the ancient *Ch'a Ching* or *Classic of Tea* by Lu Yu for whom "tea symbolized the harmony and mysterious unity of the Universe," according to one biographer.

After browsing the famous text written by the "god of tea" himself, our traveller would soon have his tea. It would come in a gleaming silver teapot to rival many of the best hotel tearooms in London, among them English Tea Room at Brown's and the Palm Court at the Ritz. He might even stay to enjoy the curry in the Bengal Lounge not far down the hall. Kipling would have been right at home, seeing large puka fans swaying from the high ceiling.

When the weary traveler had quite finished sipping and eating his fill of tea sandwiches and assorted pastries, he would be glad for the wait, happy to have feasted at the crowning glory of tearooms, possibly the best Canada has to offer.

Did the Texan achieve his goal? Alas, it seems his cruise ship had an early departure on its way to Alaska. He would have to wait again.

A King's Tea at Thanksgiving
Enjoying tea with the ghost of a former Canadian prime minister and his mother

Canada has long been under the reign of Queen Elizabeth II, but it once had its own king, or rather King. He was William Lyon Mackenzie King, the former dominion's tenth prime minister and a tea fancier judging from a Thanksgiving stroll around his expansive estate at Kingsmere near Ottawa, the Canadian capital.

One of the great delights about visiting the National Capital Region, which flows over the Quebec-Ontario boundary, is the stunning autumn foliage that blankets the area each year. As sure as the changing of the guard on the lawns of Parliament Hill attracts throngs of tourists every summer, the colourful changing of the leaves in the fall draws Ottawans and tourists alike to the Gatineau Hills a few miles north into Quebec.

The annual pilgrimage begins in early October and takes leaf lovers into handsome Gatineau Park where one passes through small towns with British-sounding names. A steam train wends its way along the picturesque Gatineau River to Wakefield, a quaint English enclave that is struggling to keep from having its named changed to *La Peche*. The language-sensitive Quebec government is ever-watchful of attempts to subvert its language law and who can blame them, living in a sea of English as they do.

Driving past the brick church and cemetery at Old Chelsea, leaf seekers are compelled to stop and marvel at the burnt oranges, crimson reds and bright yellows that frame the graveyard. Here, they can stop for morning coffee or tea and indulge in some French toast covered in locally produced maple syrup. Afterwards, peek at local artists' depictions of woodsy Canadiana in all seasons at galleries in the area.

Once past Old Chelsea, the destination of choice is Kingsmere, a two-hundred-and-thirty-one-hectare expanse of well-treed land on Kingsmere Lake. Here, prime minister King spent his leisure time while "shepherding Canada from semi-colonial status to full autonomy," as the brochure puts it. But even leisure didn't stop the industrious former labour and foreign minister from building three houses on the tree-filled terrain.

Biographies and film treatments have often portrayed King as an eccentric statesman. They depict the man who served almost twenty-two years as Canada's Liberal PM – the longest-serving – as over-dedicated to his mother even seeking her advice through a medium after her death. They have him steering Canada through the Second World War and an attendant conscription crisis, while consulting his dog Pat every step of the way.

But whatever the grandson of famed Canadian rebel William Lyon Mackenzie was in public life, his image of himself as reflected at Kingsmere was of a man of distinction, high culture and classical interests. Even the old yellow and green Kingswood cottage and guest house near the lake revealed his refined tastes.

Its broad verandah, flower pots hanging from a parabola and a boathouse cum change room, all show his careful attention to detail. A tea trolley and tea set in a dining room corner were ready to be wheeled into his high-ceilinged den with its big open fireplace and wood-panelled walls.

King had a passion for architecture revealed by his restoration of a nineteenth-century farmstead on another part of the estate. It is now the official residence of the Speaker of the House of Commons. But it was at Moorside, an elegant, two-storey building, that he entertained heads of state including Winston Churchill. And it is at Moorside that we find the tearoom.

In summer, visitors can take tea on the porch and admire the formal flower beds and a hidden rock garden. Not far away are the classical ruins that the PM reconstructed on a hill as if to create his own mini-acropolis. Straight ahead from the porch is one of many forest trails on the estate. This one takes you along a fast-flowing creek to some gentle falls, while others lead to nearby lakes or meander along tree-roofed pathways occasionally revealing valley vistas.

In fall, a walk on the trails, kicking through the fallen leaves, builds up an appetite and a thirst, two urges the Moorside Tearoom is ready and able to satisfy. You may have to wait a bit, but this allows time to tour King's living quarters on the second floor. Again, the wood panelling adds warmth as does the tea trolley centrally positioned in the former PM's large den and study.

Under new management, the tearoom now caters to visitors year round, offering salads, sandwiches, *quiche Lorraine* and *croque monsieurs*. Pastry lovers can enjoy home-made apple, pumpkin and sugar pies, a Quebec specialty. But the afternoon tea is the obvious show-stopper on the menu, and at $9.95 it's a bargain.

At Thanksgiving, the three-tiered tray appropriately includes a turkey triangle, crab and pollack on mini pita, and the more traditional English cucumber and cream cheese on dark rye. Sultana scones are served with strawberry sauce and whipped cream (clotted cream is rare in Canadian tearooms; no doubt part of the ceaseless battle against cholesterol). To finish, a generous slice of carrot cake joins a maple sugar *tartellette*.

The teas are loose (again a rarity in many Canadian tea places) and imported by the Metropolitan Tea Company. Buckingham Palace Garden Tea and Vienna Opera Ball are favourites. Other blacks on offer: Lover's Leap Pekoe, Pure Indian Darjeeling and Earl Grey. For the less orthodox: strawberry kiwi, lemon-mango, maple tea, Jasmine, Camomile, Lapsang Souchong, and a Japanese green tea called Fukujyu.

King would be disappointed to learn that the tea cream comes in plastic, the sugar in paper packets next to the paper napkins. Yellow sachets of "low-cal sweetener" come with an ominous warning that they "should be taken only on the advice of a physician."

Still, tea drinkers find themselves in cosy, if crowded, comfort surrounded by floral curtains, table bouquets, a large central fireplace, dark wood walls and many windows from which to gaze at the leafy outdoors. Who knows? As a bonus, one might even see the ghost of a prime minister...or his mother.

King came to this "restful place" to "escape the pressures of public life," says the brochure. Thankfully, Canada's National Capital Commission has allowed the rest of us to share in the simple pleasures of escape that continue to be provided at Moorside Tea-room.

Teatime in the Rockies
Where buffalo don't roam and the tea comes in bags

I'd always wanted to ride the five miles or so on horseback to take tea at what was rumoured to be a little log teahouse high above Lake Louise in Banff National Park in the Canadian Rockies. What a unique experience to add to the many I had already had in the world of tea. Now was my chance to realize that dream. I came close...sort of.

The horse was a 30-foot 1983 Pace Arrow mobile home with all the amenities. The lake was Upper Waterton Lake in Waterton Lakes National Park, a few minutes from the Alberta-Montana border. And the teahouse was the Prince of Wales Hotel overlooking the pretty tourist town of Waterton.

I say pretty but that refers largely to the unbeatable surroundings. This is as close to God's Country as it gets. It is described as the place where "the mountains meet the prairies" and it is breathtaking. But tea-lover charming it is not.

At least it isn't unless you mean the lovely white-tailed deer that wander freely through the government-run campground where we had parked our trusty metal steed for the night. Tiny chipmunks shared ground with the deer and the gophers while magpies screeched annoyingly. Rugged, perhaps; outdoorsy maybe. But hardly charming.

The town itself was two or three streets of over-priced hotels, motels, cafes (including a cappuccino bar cum born-again Christian book store and a Welch's Chocolate Shop) and numerous gift shops. The shops lined up side by side on the main street, all offering more or less the same items. There were Indian sweaters, T-shirts with bears on them, and books about the life of Kootenai Brown, an old mountain man who became the park's legendary first ranger.

You could also buy candies, not so quaintly called "Moose droppings," leather moccasins, and a bowl of buffalo and wild berry soup at Zum's, one of half a dozen local restaurants. Ice tea was on every menu and it was doing a brisk business in the hot summer weather.

I've never been a big fan of powdered Nestea even with ice in it. Rather, my pleasure lies in a good strong cup of real tea brewed from scratch using loose leaves, poured at just the right moment and let steep for the precise time limit of four minutes. Could I find it in this mountain town surrounded by peaks that are so sharp they look like God's teeth poking out of a great gaping mouthful of prairie sky?

To satisfy my craving, I had to climb a steep path through wild roses, the delightful pink symbol of Alberta, sometimes known as the Texas of Canada. This is a cattle-raising province, after all, and it is filthy rich with oil. It also has a Texas-sized reputation as redneck alley. Bible thumpers live side by side with cow punchers and oil-rig roughnecks here in Canada's socially and politically conservative heartland.

It's always useful to know what kind of environment one is about to enter as one sits for afternoon tea. And it would appear that Albertans do not put the quality of their tea very high on the list of things that 'had darn well better change around here and soon.' Of course, some things never change, especially when they draw in tourists by the busload from May to October when tea is served at the Prince of Wales.

As I waited to be seated, I stared at one of them in the hotel lobby, something as Canadian as the Rockies themselves: a Mountie in bright red tunic, rivaling the beaver as the most recognizable symbol of this vast country. There he was peering at us from beneath the famed peaked hat and a fat moustache just like in those old Nelson Eddy and Jeanette McDonald movies. It was only a painting on a sign, but he was clearly inviting me to take high tea with him, wasn't he?

"Did you see the price they're asking?" said a big man with a very red neck sitting next to the tea table set up to attract the tourists.

The sign said $24.99, $19.99 of which would be for the "unobstruct-ed southerly view" from the full floor-to-ceiling windows in that part of the lobby doubling as a tearoom.

Obviously, the red-necked man was not about to indulge. His idea of afternoon tea might well be hot water in a cup with a bag on the side and a few Ritz crackers. I hoped the Prince of Wales would do better than that.

It was an awe-inspiring setting. The president of the Great Northern Railway constructed the old building to resemble a Swiss chalet. It officially opened on July 25, 1927, with 81 rooms built on seven storeys under a steep-pitched roof. The railway man may have added the cedar furniture and some impressive chandeliers in the shape of gunmetal black chuck wagon wheels. Note that the hotel, once part of the storied Canadian Pacific Railway chain, was named after Britain's Prince Edward.

A young woman named Andrea from nearby Beaver Mines, Al-berta, seated me. Our table was near the piano on one side and an older man on the other who was busily scratching his stocking feet while he lounged in a lobby easy chair. As I waited for tea, I gazed at the spectacular Rockies, massive creatures that seemed to rise out of the lake like giant mastodons. One set of peaks looked like a huge rhinoceros head.

Andrea returned with a platter of goodies and two pots of hot water. She sashayed over to me in her tartan skirt. "We are wearing Royal Stuart tartan because it is the closest to Prince of Wales tar-tan," she explained. Then in hushed tone she added, "It's against the law to wear it." She then held out a wooden box of Twinnings tea bags. Missing, rather oddly, were both Earl Grey and English Break-fast. I was clearly meant to choose the Prince of Wales.

A young pianist was playing some Erik Satie when I first en-tered, but now she switched to lighter fare including several memo-rable tunes from *A Sound of Music* as in "The hills are alive..." She didn't play badly and by now the man with itchy feet had mercifully moved on. But the tea goodies fell far short of my expectations.

We began with the smoked salmon sandwich fingers accompanied by soggy watercress and cucumber ones, then on to a surprisingly good scone. Alongside was a too chilly pot of cream that we later learned was Somerdale English Devon Cream distributed from Toronto by Somerset. "I thought it was cream cheese," Andrea said. "But the little French girl in the kitchen – she doesn't speak much English – said it was from England. I hope you like it."

She made no apology for not serving jam. Instead, we were given lots of fresh blueberries and red seedless grapes. The other sweets included strawberry mousse in a tiny chocolate cup, two large chocolate-covered strawberries, a slice of pink raspberry cheesecake, pecan cookies, macaroons and an oval-shaped piece of maple fudge.

As I finished, the pianist said farewell with a flourish, playing *Body and Soul* and *April in Paris* before quitting for the afternoon at 4:30 p.m. on the dot.

Tea with Dinosaurs
Keemun with Saskatoon berry cobbler in the Badlands of Alberta

The 1983 Pace Arrow mobile home, a 30-foot dinosaur, lumbered through Dinoland in the heart of what was Alberta coal-mining country until the late 1940s when oil and natural gas were discovered. After that, about one hundred and twenty-five mines that operated in the region went extinct. Ever since, dinosaurs have been keeping the local economy alive and well.

Astonishingly, this is also tearoom country. Or is that so astonishing? Alberta is not just home to the remains of T Rex and company over at the world-class Royal Tyrell Museum of Paleontology, a must-stop along the highway called the Dinosaur Trail. It is also known for its conservative ways. In fact, dinosaurs are what some people call Albertans, especially the politicians that hail from there.

Now, some might say that same image fits well with tearooms, that old Victorian institution of a bygone conservative era. But it isn't a fair fit. Little tearooms are scattered across the prairie at old mining towns like Rosebud, Delia and East Coulee. And while they may not be Victoriana quaint, they are uniquely Albertan.

With a landscape that could be mistaken for a moonscape, the region is a geologist's dream-come-true. The strange rock formations carved out of the Red Deer River valley make for eye-popping and camera-snapping scenery. One area called the Hoodoos strongly resembles Cappadocia in Western Turkey with its phallic mounds thrusting toward the endless blue prairie sky.

But it is dry, dusty country, too, and that makes travelers thirsty, especially tea travelers like me. Next stop: East Coulee School Museum and the Willow Tearoom then owned and operated by Tony and Andy de Jong, originally from The Netherlands. The de Jongs quit their city jobs about six years before and decided to turn the school, opened in 1930 when the coal town had 3,000 residents, into a tourist attraction.

"I'm doing a bus tour from New Orleans next week," Tony said as she polished an item in her tea cabinet. Next door, one of the staff was acting out the role of a 1930s school marm to the delight of a gaggle of school children. Down the hall, Andy was explaining some of the articles in the mining wing of the museum.

"The miner's union was strong in these parts," he whispered secretively as I looked at old trade union photos. "Lot of communists around here then." He frowned that disapproving Alberta red-neck frown that suggested he truly believed all trade unionists report directly to some Evil Empire. Another dinosaur. Soon he was in the basement demonstrating a rig that helped him feed coal to the old boiler. Yet another dinosaur of sorts, yet it still heats the place in the sub-zero Alberta winters.

"Barbara Streisand's husband is doing his latest film up here," Andy said. "It's about two guys in a boxcar who work over at Atlas Mine." That's another dinosaur of the region that is now also a museum. The Disney people filmed Noah's Ark here and CBS has shot footage of the town and area for its film archives, Andy added.

Tony fixed tea while I was taking the grand tour and getting briefed on various dinosaurs. It was now ready. I had scanned the menu for unusual fare and ordered the blueberry rhubarb cobbler, the Willow's specialty. Tony used Saskatoon berries when they were ready for picking in late July. I also asked for a scone with boysenberry jam, but this was a mistake. It was burnt on the bottom and as flat as a pancake. I realized that flatness is a common prairie attribute, but it doesn't work with scones.

I could have had the Miner's Lunch ("For hungry people"), consisting of garlic sausage, cheddar cheese, bread, onions, sauerkraut and pickles. But I passed on it. For my cholesterol's sake, I also opted against having the "Hoo Doo hotdog." I washed out the burnt taste of the scone with a cup of Keemun bagged tea.

"I thought you might go for the Lapsang," Tony said as she bussed the table removing the blue and rose-patterned Colclough English bone china. Also on the table were tiny wooden school desks to hold the salt and pepper shakers. A small coal car held the paper napkins. Alberta quaint.

I made a short stop at the museum gift shop to examine the "dinosaur teeth" and "Albertasauros toes," then headed toward the Valley of the Dinosaurs. I might have stayed in the area for a taste of the Texas-style Baby Back Ribs ('the best you've ever tasted!") at the Mother Mountain Teahouse in Delia down the road.

Or I could have taken tea at the Rosebud Country Inn Tearoom. Then there was the That's Crafty Barn & Tearoom closer to Drumheller. They specialized in "giant cinnamon buns."

I passed on all of them. It was time to point the Pace Arrow southwards and leave the Badlands behind. But as I left East Coulee I had the distinct feeling that there would be more dinosaurs dead ahead.

Tea on Canada's Inland Sea
Looking for Rita's of Big Pond with the sun blazing and
trash Top-40 music blaring

I drove the four hours to Cape Breton Island, Nova Scotia, from the
Halifax airport with the sun blazing through the windshield at 30
Celsius. The radio was blaring Top-40 trash music as I made my
way to a little town called Big Pond whose main claim to fame is
Rita's Tearoom.

My one stop was on the outskirts of Antigonish, home to St.
Francis Xavier University and the oldest highland games on the continent. A huge sign advertised Mother Webb's Steak House. My
stomach begged me to pull over and investigate. My better judgment
advised against. The stomach won, as usual, and would suffer for it
later. The sign was the best thing about Mother Webb's. It is the
kind of café where the steaks glisten with grease and the French fries
go from freezer to bubbling fat.

I could have done my stomach a favour, left it on empty and
headed for Uncle Ron's Coffee Shop. Instead, I inflicted double
damage. How could I pass a place with my first name on the sign
even if it was a coffee shop?

I bought a large oatmeal and raisin cookie and ordered the hot-
test latte on record. Uncle Ron doesn't roast his own beans. Like a
lot of things out here, the name is a façade. Then again, what is Starbucks but a façade? At least Uncle Ron's is local.

***

I got to Big Pond at about 2 p.m., driving well over the 110 kph
speed limit most of the way. In the Cape, the limit drops to 100 kph.
Distances are indicated in miles as well as kilometres. That's another
thing about the east coast. Change isn't so easily accepted in the oldest part of Canada, especially not along the shores of Bras d'Or
Lake, "Canada's Inland Sea." While the rest of Canada went metric
years ago, Capers continued to keep the dual signage. Perhaps it was
in deference to the American tourist trade.

Rita's Tearoom was right off Highway 4, two lanes of hardtop with enough potholes to make you tea-thirsty in a region where Tim Horton donut franchises have replaced the church and the corner hardware store as the local gathering place. Maritimers are fishers, miners, bed and breakfasters. But above all they are coffee drinkers. I prided myself in knowing that I was about to take tea in what was probably the last real tearoom in Atlantic Canada.

"Hi! I'll be your server today," said the cheery voice of a forty-something waitress standing over me in her Rita's Tearoom smock. "Let me tell you how wonderful Rita is," she added without prompting. "Last Friday she wanted to shut down the tearoom for the whole day because it was the funeral of a son of one of her staff."

The Rita in question is singer/songwriter Rita MacNeil, she of CBC Television stardom, she of the big silky smooth voice that permeates the rafters of the tearoom bearing her name. Rita, a Big Pond native, has forever endeared herself to the Cape mining population with her powerful rendition of *Working Man*, a moving tune about miners and their fate.

Still, I was taken aback by the server's comment. You don't usually get this kind of effusive praise before you've even had a chance to peruse the menu. I soon learned that the tearoom was as much a hangout for Rita fans as an eatery and that at least one staff member appeared to be the fan club president.

"She's a wonderful person and a wonderful boss," the server went on. "So genuinely kind. It's the nicest place I've ever worked. But please don't tell anyone I said so."

I ordered "Rita's Afternoon Tea" and settled into the atmosphere of what the menu describes as a "one-room school house." Rita bought it in the early 1980s and raised her family here, inviting friends to drop by for tea (Rita's "favourite beverage," says the menu).

The server soon returned with a small teapot and a cup and saucer with "Rita" written in red on both. A plate held a cherry pudding tart with whipping cream adorned with chocolate sprinkles. There was also a dry cinnamon roll and an equally dry tea biscuit (not a scone). The latter resembled the dinner rolls you get at a lobster supper in church basements around these parts. The lobster suppers are popular and that year the price was running up to $21.95 in most places.

"Do you know what Devonshire Cream is?" the server asked setting down a second plate with three little pots on it. I said I did. "Well, this is our very own variety." It was a cream that poured rather than dolloped, but I kept quiet on this point as I did when I saw that there was precious little of the runny substance and that it was heavily laced with sugar.

Devonshire cream it was not. Still, "people say it's the best they have ever tasted." A ball of butter no bigger than my thumbnail sat benignly in another small pot. In the third was a small portion of strawberry jam. It too was pourable. But there was no pot of extra hot water as is the custom in many tearooms. The apparent purpose is to squeeze another cup out of the spent tea bag. Gratefully, I had no need of it.

The tea was Rita's Tearoom Blend. "People say it's the best they've ever tasted," said the server sounding repetitive, but no one could tell me who did the blending except that it was a mixture of "orange and black Pekoe."

"Rita used to live in this part of the tearoom," said another staff member who was greeting people at the door. An old stove, radio and clock sat on a hearth near the tea trolley at the entrance. "She and the kids, Laura and Wade." Laura was managing the tearoom at the time while Wade managed Rita's singing career.

The career took off in the 1980s with songs like *Flying On Your Own*, which some consider to be her biggest hit, and albums like *Reason to Believe*. A room full of memorabilia testifies to her grand successes. Photos of her paper the walls. There she is posing with Anne ("Snowbird") Murray, Bruce Cockburn, Buffy Sainte-Marie, Joni Mitchell, even the Queen. Raffi, the celebrated children's songster, Tommy Hunter, another Maritime country-singing legend, the Rankin Family and the Barra-MacNeils are there, along with gold and platinum records, honourary degrees and Rita's trademark red hat.

Over at the shop, almost everything had Rita written, carved, embroidered, painted or etched on it. One can buy Rita letter openers, paper weights, pewter spoons, aprons, tote bags, wristwatches, earrings, key chains, T-shirts, baseball caps, fleece jackets and a tea biscuit mix. Of course, there was an array of Rita tea things as well: sugar bowls, creamers, cozies, tea bag holders, mugs, cups, saucers, teapots.

Rita was everywhere. Her voice wafted softly from speakers spread around the tearoom. Her photo smiled at you from posters. Out on the new patio, part of the expansion in 1994, her name was on the green umbrellas. Her songs were embroidered on wall hangings by artist Carol MacLean as is her Member of the Order of Canada certificate.

But Rita in person was nowhere to be found. "Oh, she's around," said one of the staff members. "She has a summer home in Big Pond but she lives in Sydney [N.S.]. You never know when she'll pop by."

As I was finishing the last of my liquidy Devonshire cream, I had to conclude that there was one sure thing about Rita's Tearoom: it knew how to promote Rita's Tearoom. And the promotion apparently had paid off.

"We get 40,000 visitors a year," said the staff member confidently. The season ran from June 1 to October 15 and the tearoom had been open for fifteen seasons at the time of my visit.

Even that year, when many Cape Breton merchants were complaining that the tourist traffic was way down, the staffer stood her ground. Locals say it's because of the high gas prices, the bad weather (rain and more rain everywhere), and inexplicably the American election.

I sat looking out at Grand Bras d'Or Lake through a mullioned window with dark green curtains to match the green upholstery on the chairs. The curtains were a floral pattern and the chairs were covered in grapes and vines. It was chintz-like but not chintz.

"You go past MacLeod's store across from the homemade fishcakes stand and all the way to Chippin Dale's Fish and Chips," the staff member instructed me as I was leaving Rita's. "That's the one in the boat by the junction for Highway 4 and Highway 216."

She mapped out my route through Eskasoni, the largest Mi'kmaq Indian reserve in Nova Scotia. "They're very poor but they're nice people," she said apologetically. "We've got one of the boys working here with us."

The CJFX announcer had just finished "interviewing" another local businessman. "It's a hot one today!" he said in the nasal voice, the one that must have been standard issue at all broadcasting schools back then. Rita's voice was the next thing I heard as I drove on.

Hollywood High Tea
At the Beverly Hills Hotel with the ghost of Howard Hughes, Marilyn and maybe Charlie Chaplin

It was a few days after the Academy Awards and I was snuggled into a high-backed easy chair at the Sunset Tea Lounge in posh Beverly Hills hoping for a glimpse of some Oscar winners along with my Hollywood high tea.

"Warren Beatty, Annette Bening and their children were sitting right over there last week," said a junior staff member, all excited. "Just before Ms. Bening won the Oscar for her role in *American Beauty*. She said they came here to relax and get away from the crowds."

There were certainly no crowds that day, although rumours were flying that some hugely successful Hollywood producer was dining on the private patio next door. Of course, that happens in LaLa Land. Everyone seems to be craning their necks to see a star. The rumours proved false, by the way; it was some rich executive from Saatchi and Saatchi.

City bus No. 204 runs along Sunset Boulevard through famed Sunset Strip, making me flash back to that early television show, *77 Sunset Strip*, with Ed "Cookie" Burns and Efrem Zimbalist Jr. It's famous for clubs like the Whisky-A-Go-Go, where the Doors and Jimi Hendrix performed, and Johnny Depp's Viper Room where Keanu Reeves can be heard with his band Dogstar.

Not far from where the No. 204 picked me up, I was trying to fit my hands into those of Humphrey Bogart at Mann's Chinese Theatre and strolling the "Walk of Stars" to gaze at the 2,000-plus names inserted into the sidewalk.

Tea was a welcome and soothing antidote to the TV-show-ticket floggers, tourists and trinket shops, the latter selling last-week's Oscar memorabilia and whatever else Silver Screen star-gazers are willing to buy.

When we finally got to Beverly Hills – note to others: prepare to spend a lot of time in a vehicle when you come to LA – it was like leaving *The Day of the Locusts* and moving into *Beverly Hills 90210,* the popular teen TV soap of the day.

Hollywood is "so five minutes ago," someone once said. But Beverly Hills, with its hidden millionaires' mansions, quiet palm-studded streets and over-abundance of Mercedes Benz convertibles, is up-to-date, establishment chic.

Then there is the old Beverly Hills Hotel, with its bungalows and its park-like surroundings. It seems to epitomize the lifestyles of Beverly Hills residents like Jack Nicholson, Harrison Ford, Sandra Bullock, and the Beatty/Benings. You can't help but relax and soak up the atmosphere of Tinsel Town history as you enter the grounds of this old haunt of the stars.

Marlene Dietrich sang at the Polo Lounge in 1940. Howard Hughes set up housekeeping in one of the bungalows in 1942 and stayed there off and on for thirty years. Marilyn Monroe and Yves Montand slept in bungalows 20 and 21 during the filming of *Let's Make Love* in 1959. Gregory Peck and Lauren Bacall made *Designing Women* here in 1957. Charlie Chaplin roomed here when he got a special Oscar in 1972.

The whole place oozes stardom and I was as keen a star-gazer as any teabag tourist ever was. "Isn't that Mel Gibson over there at the main desk?" I said. "That's Cuba Gooding Jr. over there by the fountain, isn't it?" It might have been, too, but I didn't take time to check. I was equally anxious to settle into a comfy corner of the lounge and order Sunset's $20 afternoon tea. I could have added Roederer Estate Anderson Valley 'Brut' champagne, a Fonseca Bin #27 Port or a Grand Marnier for $24. But I wanted to say razor-sharp in case a star entered the same orbit I was travelling in.

The server soon delivered a three-tiered array of savoury items, including egg salad with watercress, sweet chicken salad on marble rye, European cucumber with dill cream, fresh asparagus with Boursin cheese and Scottish smoked salmon on pumpernickel. It all looked fabulous but tasted like it had just come out of the refrigerator – dry and tasteless.

My tea choice was the hotel's private blend of Orange Pekoe and black tea (the menu didn't say which black tea). It could have been Assam, Darjeeling, Earl Grey Supreme or English Breakfast. Also on offer were Fanciest Formosa Oolong, Temple of Heaven Gunpowder, Sencha, Jasmine and a variety of herbal teas. Harney and Sons (1-800-teatime) supplied the lot.

A second triple-tier carried the sweets: atomic-sized chocolate-dipped strawberries on the top tier, fruit and lemon tarts, zucchini and apple-walnut breads along with macaroons on the second, and dry, too-light scones on the bottom one. I gobbled it all off of Wedgewood's 'Clio' with its colourful berries and flowers pattern. Evelyn and Crabtree jams came in small jars. Somerdale Double Devon Cream, also in one-ounce jars, was an unexpected treat that made me partially forgive the tearoom for serving sub-quality scones.

When asked, the second server was reluctant to say which stars frequented the hotel. "It's really breaking hotel policy to tell you," she said apologetically. But we knew I was in the midst of Hollywood stardom. I could just feel that I was surrounded by the aura of Big Screen greatness, secluded here under the tall palms of Will Rogers Park across Sunset Boulevard.

From my spotless starchy white-napped table I stretched to see if that really was Kevin Spacey or Nicole Kidman standing near the bodyguard at the entrance to the men's room outside the Sunset Tea Lounge of Beverly Hills in the city of plastic dreams.

***

Of course, this is California, flaky, tacky, trendy California. So, a tea trip to Hollywood wouldn't be complete without adding in something off-beat. Are you ready for a "ZenFusion" at the Zen Zoo Tearoom in Brentwood? Huh?

"The history of Zen Zoo Tea is about more than just the creation of a teahouse," says the Zen Zoo web site. "It is about the dedication of its founders to reinvent the corporation as an instrument that encourages individuals to create, achieve and realize their goals and dreams." Now is that California enough for you or what?!

The owners started Zen Zoo in the Year of the Tiger in hopes that it "would embody the spirit of the Asian teahouse while satisfying the need for balance in our modern society." They intended to "create an environment that is distinctively Zen Zoo Tea and reflects the concept's energy, excitement and commitment to quality."

I figured the web site writer might have been high on a special blend of California-grown tea when he added that "Big dreams can come true. We invite you to come and realize your dreams at Zen Zoo Tea – the place where life happens."

Woah! That's getting a bit carried away. There's a lot of philosophy there and not a lot of tea. What the place offered that was unique was ZenFusion, a "shake tea" now widely known as bubble tea. It's described on the menu as a "fruit infused ice tea drink prepared 'martini style'."

The owners can keep all the mumbo jumbo about Asian teahouses and corporate balance. Fortified for the sunny LA weather by a tea martini, I struck out toward Pacific Palisades and down the Pacific Coast Highway to Malibu. The Beach Boys were blaring from the car radio.

What the Calico Cat Saw
Psychic mystery at a tea-leaf reading flavoured with lime-layered Nanaimo bars

A baby husky greeted me in the parking lot of the Calico Cat Tea-house in Nanaimo, British Columbia. He was clean, furry and friendly. I was cautious...and not just because husky's can be unpredictable. This was to be my first experience with a *bona fide* tea-leaf reader – a tasseographer – so I was expectantly nervous.

Nanaimo, a busy coastal town and ferry terminal on the east coast of Vancouver Island, is the second largest island community next to the capital city of Victoria. It is a pensioner's heaven if you can dismiss persistent rumours that the Hell's Angels have taken over the local economy.

The Calico Cat is slightly out of town, just a whisker from the seaside and a cat's meow from the multi-laned highway that carries traffic south to bedroom communities like Ladysmith and Chemainus and north to retirement havens at Parksville and Qualicum Beach.

I said "nice doggie" to the husky and moved slowly around to the entrance where I was greeted by Muleah, a young woman with a floppy ponytail.

"Is everything okay, sir?" she asked, escorting me to a small table. I said it was and ordered afternoon tea, a bargain at $12.95 considering the prices charged in Victoria tearooms about ninety minutes south on the mountainous and wintery Malahat Highway.

The famed Empress Hotel charged $42 in those days for the privilege of taking tea in its Tea Lobby. The equally famed Butchart Gardens, a few miles out of the capital, served as good an afternoon or high tea at half the price. But you paid a $10 fee for the added pleasure of the surrounding one-hundred-year-old botanical gardens.

The Calico Cat wasn't offering quite as extravagant an eating experience, but you could have both breakfast and lunch there. "Our famous crepes" were available, for example, or "home-made mushroom soup…with a touch of white wine." There was also Cornish pastie or a ploughman's lunch with English trifle for dessert. And it seemed that almost everything could include asparagus.

Afternoon tea was described on the menu as "a delightful presentation of dainty sandwiches, sweets, fruits, and our famous scones, all homemade in our teahouse kitchen by our wonderful cooks." I ordered it in anticipation as soft classical guitar music washed through my little room.

In my little room was my little round table with pink covering under floral green and wine-coloured overlay. There was a paper placemat with holly printed on it. A pair of 'greasy spoon' salt and pepper shakers sat near the square purple vase that held a sparse arrangement of dried flowers. Next to it was a no-name creamer and sugar bowl, the kind you might buy in the same shop that sells ceramic lawn ornaments.

A whirring overhead fan had three ornate light fixtures clinging to it. Modern, leaded stain glass had been fitted into the windows above me. Aging lace curtains were drawn back and held with a Christmas ribbon. The walls were spotted with framed Victorian prints of children and tranquil settings in the forest.

I looked at the flat paper Rudolph by the door. Other Christmas decorations were festooned about the main floor of the high-ceilinged old house. Plastic evergreen boughs hung over most doorways. A teddy bear sat in a small wooden wheelbarrow with a sign in it offering this advice: "Never eat more than you can lift."

The fireplace in the centre of the largest room had a display of biblical figurines on the mantel. Christmas stockings made of lambskin hung from it. Teacups and saucers, pots and porcelain dolls were stacked on every available shelf.

Muleah brought my tea and placed a monster brownie in front of one of the two young women who also occupied my little room. They paused to stare then went back to talking about their clerks' jobs and dreaming aloud about getting married.

Mine was a two-tiered food tray. The top tier held finger sandwiches – egg, cheese with chopped scallions on brown (no shrimp or salmon although a shrimp and, of course, asparagus crepe were available). The tier was garnished with kiwifruit, orange slices and a sprig of parsley.

The bottom tier held one of the Calico Cat's "famous" scones with a maraschino cherry toothpicked to it. Two small bowls contained sweet lemon curd and whipped cream. The tier also held a small piece of lemon cake, a macaroon square and the ubiquitous Nanaimo bar (after all, this was Nanaimo). The latter had a layer of creamy lime-filling. Garnishing the lot, strangely, were two half-slices of tomato.

"Is everything O.K., sir?" Muleah asked me again as she was clearing the remains of the monster brownie next door. Again I said it was as my tea-leaf reader joined me.

***

Kim came dressed in black. "I am a spiritual adviser, really," she said when I asked how one became a tasseographer. Heather, Calico's owner, normally did the readings. She "combines her own intuition with a traditional knowledge of the art learned at her grandmother's knee," the take-away menu said. "A reading with our resident reader will inspire and enlighten you, answer your questions, and amaze you with its accuracy, imagery, and wisdom." Heather's reputation as "a wise, humourous, caring and insightful tea-leaf reader" was apparently "well-earned." Alas, this was her day off.

Kim billed herself as more than a mere tea-leaf reader. She was a "medium, a clairvoyant, clairsentient and clairaudient." I had to ask what those things meant and what they had to do with getting my tea leaves read.

When I asked if there was a reference text on tea-leaf reading, she said, "I suppose there is a book, many books, I'm sure." But she didn't know of any. Clearly tea-leaf reading was far down her list of skills. One of these was making contact with dead loved ones.

"I have a lot of touch with guardian angels," she said. "I'm also channeling. You can turn me on and tune me in like a radio. I just pass on information that I've been given. I sometimes walk up to people in the street and bring them a message from a loved one. They look at me like I'm crazy but sometimes I get a call months later saying I was right."

With that she activated a portable tape recorder she had placed on the table. "I tape the readings in case you want to listen to it again when you go home." She then asked me to overturn my Royal Osborne tea cup into its saucer, put my hand on top and make a wish. I wished for world peace and an end to world hunger.

"Two angels are beside you right now," she began. "Hmmm. Interesting. I see a yes for your wish, but you know patience is one of the…. Do you find yourself being impatient sometimes?" I did but wanted to give her the benefit of the doubt.

"You've got changes coming in your life…I've got so many tea leaves on one side of your cup." It was true that all the leaves had bunched up leaving a small hill of brown with no other shapes at all except what might be construed as a tiny anthill or pile of mouse dung.

I was under no illusion that this was a real tea-leaf reading. I wasn't even sure that Kim knew how to read leaves. But being naturally suspicious of anyone who claims to be able to predict the future, I was curious to see what she would do with the precious little information I had volunteered.

"I've got some changes coming in your life," she went on in earnest. "And I've got a move. It comes on very strong." Okay, so I was thinking of buying a condo. If only I could find one in Vancouver or Victoria that didn't spell penury for the rest of my days.

"I'm being shown a book for you, something you've thought about since you were fourteen or fifteen. It's an old book." I had told her that I write, but not what kind of writer. Still, I hadn't a clue what she was talking about.

"I'm being shown stories. These stories are being passed down to you by some people. You need to put these stories on paper." A muse…just what every struggling writer hopes for, a muse to tell me what to write and maybe even how to write it.

"I get an auntie coming through quite strong for you. Who is this auntie that used to tell you stories?" Here Kim has gone way out on a limb. There is no such auntie, but I nod encouragingly.

"Has your mother passed?" she asks. I was having trouble with the word 'passed'. It always sounded to me like something that happened in a bathroom. One passes things that don't agree with them like kidney stones. She died almost thirty years ago and I haven't heard from her since, I replied.

"I've got this real strong sensation at the back of my head from your mom. Was she ill before she passed?" Never say die seems to be the working motto here. "Something to do with her head. It's tingling for me. It's that part of the head that if we fell on it, it would kill us instantly. She's showing me that." My mother died of a stroke, not a fall on the head. But what the heck.

"Oh, look at that," Kim's ring-laden fingers are tapping quickly on the tablecloth. "Look what your mom makes me do. Why? She keeps wanting me to bring up food with you. 'Please don't get too busy and forget to eat, son,' she says." Now Mom, you know eating too little was never my problem. I never forget to eat and had the belly to prove it.

"I have great success and prosperity for you but it doesn't come until you get more balance in your life. Does that make sense to you?" Of course it makes sense. It's what everyone hopes to hear about the future. It's what they pay money to hear. And it's what every fortune-teller has told the hopeful listener since fortune telling began. Oh, excuse me, I meant spiritual adviser.

"Your mom keeps showing me that we have to have roots." Kim turned off the tape at that point. She explained that for $13.50 I could buy a ten-minute tape recording of the reading. She passed me her business card, saying that I could call her for more insights. "I also do readings in Vancouver, Victoria and Seattle."

"Is everything okay, sir?" Muleah asked a final time as Kim was moving on to the next customer, the next lonely soul looking for his or her future in a tea cup.

The Boston Tea Party That Wasn't
Baseball and Boston cream pie with bagged Orange Pekoe

We were a few days away from the season opener at Fenway Park and I had taken to haughtily bragging that the Toronto Blue Jays were going to murder the Boston Red Sox. I was too late for tickets to the game except if I crossed the palm of a scalper with a couple of hundred greenbacks. So I had set my heart on a spot of revolutionary tea at the Boston Tea Party Museum.

The Boston Tea Party conjures up all sorts of images from the historic past but as all American schoolchildren know, it wasn't about tea at all. Rather, it was about a tax on tea and the rebellion against it that led to the founding of the United States of America.

Given the significance of this most celebrated of all tea parties, I was puzzled not to be able to find a single quality tearoom in the old east-coast city taking advantage of that history-changing event. My only hope had been the museum tearoom, but it was closed for renovations.

As a consolation prize, I took afternoon tea at the Parker House Hotel in downtown Boston where expatriate American novelist Henry James might have shared a pot with fellow writers Henry David Thoreau and Ralph Waldo Emerson. But if James were alive today, he would spend more than a few hours trying to find his restful "ceremony" in Beantown.

Parker House, now called the Omni Parker House, offers an over-chilled Boston cream pie with a pot of bagged Orange Pekoe. The hotel boasts that it invented the chocolate-covered cake that has become Massachusetts's official dessert. But don't expect that teatime will be tranquil at OPH's The Last Hurrah. This is Kennedy country and the hotel bar is cooking with political gossip.

Speaking of political cooks, if you had been at the OPH for tea in 1915, Ho Chi Minh might have prepared it. The beloved Communist leader of North Vietnam worked in the hotel's kitchen back then. And, in the 1940s, your busboy could have been future black activist Malcolm X.

But these days Boston does not offer tea drinkers much of anything "agreeable," as James put it. I'm sure I'm not the only one that might have enjoyed the Jamesian ceremony as a way of celebrating the greatest tea party of them all. Then again, I've become quite particular when it comes to tea.

***

Now that I've finished whinging, let me tell you about a tea that I did have, one of which James might have approved. But it wasn't served in a tearoom. It was at the Isabella Stewart Gardner Museum Cafe.

Our Cuban waiter (born in Miami of Cuban parents) boasted that the "Citrus Pound Cake" with "orange blossom ice cream and nasturtium syrup" was very tasty. "We use the flowers from the hanging nasturtiums in the courtyard," she added. "In addition to their dramatic beauty," said the café menu, "nasturtium blossoms were favored for culinary use in 17th-century Europe in Mediterranean-style cuisine."

I ate the tasty blossoms with gusto and delighted in an excellent cup of tea made from loose leaves supplied by MEMs, a local tea importer. I didn't notice whether they served Boston Harbour Tea by Davison Newman & Co. That's the same company whose tea got dumped into the harbour a couple of centuries ago.

Still licking my lips of the last drops of nasturtium syrup, I entered the luscious Italianate courtyard nearby. At the entrance, I stood awed by the sight of a wall-sized oil of a club scene with dancers and musicians playfully enjoying a night of revelry. It was Boston painter John Singer Sargent's *El Jaleo*.

The Gardner is a gem of an art museum, offering works by many great artists – Titian, Botticelli, Whistler, Matisse, Manet, Rubens and Rembrandt. Sargent is also well represented. The top portrait painter of his day patterned one of his portraits of Mrs. Gardner after his famous Madame X.

Most of Sargent's portraits are of the wealthy, and all of the women look like they could well afford afternoon tea with James. But Madame X caused a furor because originally the artist had painted her with a shoulder strap missing from her revealing dress. The sensuous painting of a French society woman created a scandal back in 1884. It was clearly too risqué for the day even in Paris and he had to stop painting it and restore the strap to its rightful place. He soon moved to London.

Of course, the Gardner is known for a scandal all of its own. This one is not so risqué but equally intriguing. In 1990, thieves made away with thirteen of the gallery's most treasured works, including a Rembrandt and a Vermeer. If she had been alive, no doubt Mrs. G. could have used a strong cuppa after that ordeal.

***

I continued my tea search the following day, hoping to find a tearoom near Harvard and lucked upon a Tealuxe in Brattle Square near one of the most famous universities in the world. A Tealuxe twin can be found downtown on Newbury Street, where shoppers with fat wallets and purses can buy antiques and designer clothing.

You can get a tremendous array of teas at these fast-tea shops, including the high-grade Golden Tippy Assam, Keemun Hao Ya, Tiger Hill Nilgiri and Makaibari Second Flush Darjeeling. But you are still in a rushed, frantic atmosphere not unlike what you find at a Starbucks or the home-grown Canadian chains, Tim Hortons and Second Cup.

Dado Tea, on Massachusetts Avenue and elsewhere, was providing some competition for Tealuxe. One could get loose teas there along with bubble teas, iced teas, herbal teas and house specialties like Eight Treasure Tea, Green Tea Latte and Thai Tea. You could also get an espresso, Vietnamese coffee and smoothies. But it was another fast-tea shop with even less atmosphere than Tealuxe.

After indulging in a Tealuxe Kashmiri chai ("loaded with cardamom, peppermint and nutmeg"), I took the No. 77 bus back along Massachusetts Avenue to what I thought might be the cream of Boston tearooms, Tea Tray in the Sky. My *Eyewitness* guidebook said it served a high tea and that its "renowned pastry chef makes sure the food matches the tea in quality."

I suppose I could have gone to the Bristol Lounge at the Four Seasons. *Eyewitness* said it served a "lovely tea." I could have taken tea at the Ritz-Carlton where they would have served me their "swan-boat shaped, cream-filled puff pastry." As mentioned earlier, I had wanted to visit the tearoom at the Boston Tea Party Museum. But I didn't want tourist-trap tea served in one of those metal pots that invariably leak. I hope that's not what they offer when the museum reopens.

As Bus 77 neared Tea Tray in the Sky, my mouth watered in anticipation. But it was to prove as allusive as the Da Vinci Code. There was no tearoom at No. 392. I did see a Bruegger's Bagel Bakery across the busy street where I ordered a bottle of "Squeezed Nantucket Nectars." It was called "Half and Half" (lemonade and ice tea) a.k.a. an Arnold Palmer for some reason.

When I had finished, I asked if I could make a local call. The clerk gestured to the wall phone. I tried the Tea Tray number. Not in service. I was tempted to tear that page out of *Eyewitness*, but didn't. My own fault for buying a guide that was two years out of date.

Oh, give me a classy tearoom in this historic city, I cried. Walk me along Freedom Trail until I find a tea table covered in fine starched white linen possibly embroidered by a daughter of the American Revolution. Serve me a quality tea in a replica of a silver teapot etched by silversmith Paul Revere. Yes, the same one who rode the countryside shouting, "The British are coming."

I was so frustrated that I was ready to start a revolution of my own. Maybe the absence of tearooms is what you get for staging the most famous tea party of them all, I mused vengefully.

Happily, the Toronto Blue Jays beat the Boston Red Sox the night I left town. Never mind 'give me liberty or give me death', Boston. Give me a proper tearoom or I'll keep on jinxing your Sox!

Tea in the Big Apple
Still a tearoom in NYC among Jewish delis and cafes for peanut butter lovers and Harley Davidson riders

Where to get a 'proper' afternoon tea in the Big Apple? The Palm Court at the Park Plaza offers one and you can walk off the extra pounds in Central Park afterwards. So does Leona Helmsley's around the corner with a tea leaf reading tossed in. The Cocktail Terrace at the Waldorf Astoria lets you sip a cuppa next to Cole Porter's piano.

But don't expect it from the Algonquin where Dorothy Parker and her New Yorker crowd held court at the round table (actually it was square) in the old days. And do not get your hopes up about having high tea with blintzes at the Russian Tearoom. They weren't serving it the last time I popped in.

In fact, if you work up a thirst walking the Great White Way or the Museum Mile and plan to quench it by flipping to "Tearooms" in the four-inch thick New York City Yellow Pages, get ready for a shock. There is only one listing: T Salon & Teaporium.

The big hotels compete for originality with the Waldorf, which was offering an "exceptional jasmine tea served in a cognac glass for your amazement – beautiful little pearls of green and white tea." The Park Plaza had caviar blinis with its high tea. Even the kids can join in with a chocolate-mint or vanilla tea.

But the real tearoom experience, the genuine article, was still promised at the T Salon. It was a thirst-inducing walk towards Midtown Manhattan from Greenwich Village with its jazz clubs and trattorias. But when I arrived, what was once a superb tearoom had been sadly replaced by one of those Bolshi-chic cafés that were sweeping through the West, bearing names like Pravda, Bulgaria and Lenin.

***

I was so looking forward to another visit to T. The first time I did so, I was seated in front of a perfectly brewed cup of Mariage

Frères Marco Polo in the basement of the Guggenheim Museum (SoHo).

T was a tiny treasure hidden amidst the coffee-drenched din of Manhattan. Just off Broadway at Prince and Mercer Streets, this bustling tearoom was all but lost to the unaware passerby. I had read about it in *Conde Nast Traveler* where it was described as a "Zen-like space." So I knew what I was looking for and refused to let a wicked late-autumn rain thwart me from reaching my destination.

I got waylaid by a brief visit to the museum itself which featured an exhibition called "Japan Art After 1945: Scream Against the Sky." But I was after tea, as well as art, so I quickly found and descended the steps leading to the museum basement and the delights of T.

The immediate impression was one of chaos, but perhaps that is just New York. Crowds of people were lined up waiting to be seated. Others were hoisting trays of food above their heads as they searched for a spot in a cozy dining area near the entrance. There was the usual clatter of plates and the chatter of hungry eaters at lunchtime.

I made my way past the potted plants and magazine rack, with its sizeable collection of *New Yorkers*, to the reservation podium where a young woman told me I would have a twenty-minute wait. She invited me to browse through a range of tea paraphernalia to the right of the entrance.

I accepted and found all manner of tea things seemingly strewn about on the floor as if to invite patrons to place them neatly back where they belonged. This must be New York where casual merges with the crazy.

I was helped by a young man to smell my way through several teas imported from the famed Mariage Frères tearoom in Paris. They were stored in large round tins lining the back of the long smelling table. I bought two ounces, the minimum, of Yunnan Imperial at $6.

Teapots and cups were nicely displayed in glass cases. I carefully fondled a cup made in Brazil that had been glazed in dazzlingly bright colours. I snooped behind the display to catch a glimpse of the Mariage Frères shipping crates.

Just then, the young tea server rounded the corner to catch me studying the writing on one of the tea crates. "I've found a table for you, sir," she said. "It's in the back room, away from the crowd, I'm afraid."

"That's just fine," I replied, recalling what T owner Miriam Novalle had told *Conde Nast Traveler.* "Tea is quiet and coffee is loud."

I was grateful for the quiet before returning to the rush and tumble of Broadway. I settled in with a cup of Marco Polo, described on the menu as having a "very studied bouquet." It was timed to perfection, using an egg timer, and had a sweet, fruity taste a bit like Earl Grey. It was the perfect match to my black currant scone and some peach preserves.

And it was the perfect end to a long wet walk down The Great White Way in search of Whitman's *Open Road* somewhere amidst the highways of neon, concrete canyons and rivers of shoppers and street watchers.

***

Alas, my hopes of a repeat of the fine tea experience had now been dashed. I should have been more observant. When I found it in the Yellow Pages, the new address was clearly noted as 11 E. 20th Street.

Julie Novalle, the new T owner, was the daughter of founder Miriam Novalle (French origins but Julie didn't want to talk about it). She lived in Brooklyn "where you can actually find an apartment that allows you to avoid hearing the flush of your neighbour's toilet."

An Asian couple and a gaggle of school girls passed us as she talked, but business was hardly booming as it was on my previous visit to the old location. Soon Emmanuel, the waiter from London, joined us. He was waiting to become a member of the actors guild, waiting to be discovered on or even off off Broadway.

He recommended against the Gramercy Blend that had recently changed to the Soho Blend. Instead, he wanted me to try the Ceylon Pettiagalla OP because of its "delightful vanilla flavour" and I agreed to be a tea guinea pig. He accepted my friend's order of Darjeeling and brought her the Lingia FTGFOPI. You could buy these and about two hundred others in the "Teaporium" at the entrance.

They were no longer using a small egg timer to make sure the tea was brewed to perfection. But Emmanuel assured me it was perfectly brewed. Just no timer. He couldn't remember when there were timers. Nor could Julie.

"The T Salon and Teaporium...has become a Mecca for those searching for peace and serenity amongst the bustle of New York City," claimed an information sheet Julie gave me. It is where "lovers, friends, business colleagues, and families come to enjoy great teas." Alas, the new T was not about to live up to its namesake's reputation.

The new T's tea included two scones with Devon cream, plum preserves, and tea sandwiches (smoked chicken with avocado mayo spread, red peppers and orange, triple-decker smoked salmon with black pepper cream cheese and spicy sprouts. As well, my friend and I had pecan raisin bread sandwiches with goat cheese, red radish, cucumbers and watercress, finishing with "Our signature tea cookies," Earl Grey chocolate cake, fresh strawberries, apples and honeydew melon delicately sliced and arranged Thai-style.

Teacups and saucers were nondescript ware labelled Lenox Décor University Place. The dessert plates were by Crownford of the United Kingdom, an uninspired floral pattern. The silverware was Korean stainless.

The unmatched teapots made it three strikes and you're out as the World Series drew to a close that week in NYC. In fact, everything was unmatched from start to finish. Charming for some, possibly, but not a "proper" tea by many standards including my own.

It had a Big Apple price tag at the time as well: $28 plus tax and tip. You paid for the intimate atmosphere and the Novalle touches: a series of framed Oriental etchings, several statues placed here and there, an arrangement of dry orange flowers set off by a small orange teapot in a basket.

Emmanuel hailed us a cab when we had finished. As we rushed towards La Guardia airport, the voice of Yo-Yo Ma blasted through the taxi. It was a taped message of some sort from the cab company. When we got to the airport, another Yo-Yo Ma message told us not to forget any personal items. We wondered if he might have left a cello or two behind at some point in his career. We also wondered why he needed to sell his voice to the Yellow Cab Company.

You would think a city that can support something as special-ized as the Peanut Butter and Company Cafe or one for Harley Da-vidson riders could also do the same for a quality tearoom. But obvi-ously tearooms had fallen on hard times on the east coast. The west coast, on the other hand, seemed to be ushering in a tearoom renais-sance of sorts in those days.

Tea in Frisco
Gin joints, chop houses and, yes, the odd very pleasant tea-room

I took tea at the Imperial Tea Court in the heart of San Francisco's Chinatown after my tour of the most infamous and famous prison in the United States, Alcatraz. It was intended as a quiet, restful escape from The Rock and all its nastiness.

For days I had been roaming old hippy haunts in the Haight-Ashbury district, searching for my youth as much as for quality tea-rooms, I suppose. There was Janis Joplin's apartment. People's Park was empty but started a flow of memories anyway. Digger House and the Free Clinic were well identified. Signs of 1967's Summer of Love were still visible and I wallowed in the memories that they re-ignited.

I had also walked North Beach, stopping at Vesuvius, a popular pub with the Beat crowd of Jack Kerouac and Allen Ginsberg. Right across the alley, I combed through the tight shelves of Lawrence Ferlinghetti's City Lights Books. Francis Ford Coppola's Zeotrope Studios building sat like a huge exclamation mark at the base of a street lined with trendy Italian coffee shops.

Entering the Imperial was akin to walking into an electric Kool-Aid acid otherworld. Bird cages, with birds in them, dangled from the ceiling. Lovely painted porcelain cups lined the shelves near the dark wood tables and chairs. But for the distant ring of the cable car wobbling along busy streets, I could have been hallucinating that I was in Hong Kong.

The cups were redolent of those I had used there or in Beijing and Shanghai. It was proof that the Imperial was working hard to be authentic. The shop was orderly. Ceramic pots, cups and other goods were neatly and sometimes symmetrically arranged.

When my Keemun mao feng tea arrived, I was both thirsty and famished. My stomach growled when I saw that my snack consisted of a few almonds (in the shell) and a handful of lime-green pumpkin seeds.

The server poured hot water into my cup and let it sit for a moment before dumping it into a deep metal platter that she had placed on the table. She then scooped loose tea into my cup and offered me a chance to smell the dry leaves. After filling my cup, she placed the small metal kettle on a one-ring electric burner near the table and shuffled off behind the tea counter.

Once I got the hang of holding both the saucer and the lid in one hand, I was away. The tea was delicious and totally refreshing. But the place was empty except for a young woman who engaged one of the servers, a co-owner, in a discussion.

"How long have you and your husband been working here?" she asked.

"About ten years," the co-owner said. "It's sometimes weird being together all the time." It was the lament of someone who had doubts.

"I'm trying to figure out what kind of business I could start with my husband," the woman said. "He works as an architectural consultant for the opera. He's away a lot."

It might have been the beginning of a segment on the Jerry Springer show or a Harlequin Romance novel. It was fully in San Francisco character for two strangers to strike up a conversation about something quite personal in this friendly west-coast city.

***

After lunch the next day, I hopped the cable car at the top of Lombard Street and rode through to Powell station where I caught the J train to the Noe Valley, passed Dolores Mission Park. There I would take tea at Lovejoy's Antiques and Tearoom.

Lovejoy's is quite the cornerful. It's snuggled into the corner of Church and Clipper Streets in one of the city's high-earner neighbourhoods. A tree provided shade and a false sense that I was entering an English cottage somewhere in the Cotswolds.

Two brown poodles lolled at the front door when I arrived, seeming to lend credence to my assumption that this was a well-to-do part of town. An old wooden lectern greeted me as I walked across the threshold. All around me, arranged in a cluttered English country garden way, were chintz chairs, teapots and teacups. Trivets shaped like teapots hung from several walls. Teaspoon collections sat mutely in their cases on other walls.

A Japanese foursome sat in white lace-covered chairs at a low table lit by a single bulb cloaked in a pink Victorian-era lampshade. The woman seemed to have her cell phone surgically inserted in her left ear.

I wasn't very hungry after having indulged in one of Molinari's hearty sandwiches over in North Beach. But I felt compelled to try the cream tea anyway. It came on a single plate adorned with fresh fruit – sliced apples, oranges and pineapple wedges, two fat blackberries and an even fatter strawberry.

The tea, a black from Taylors of Harrogate, arrived in an unlabelled teapot. It had not been properly timed and so hadn't steeped long enough. The rest of the teaware was unmatched (the cup was a Noritake), and the silverware was made in China.

Now to the true test...the scones. They were too spongy for my taste, and the jam was too sweet although it had an edible lavender flower covering it. The good news: real Devonshire cream. Not whipped cream as I had come to expect of North American tearooms.

Lovejoy's probably wasn't worth the twisty J-train ride except for one non-culinary discovery. That was Ulrica Hume's book, *San Francisco in a Teacup – A Guide for Tea Lovers*. It offered "50 unique places to have tea in S.F. and the Bay area."

What does Ulrica have to say about Lovejoy's? She called it a "quirky neighbourhood tearoom." One of the owners was a "gifted psychic." But I'm afraid it didn't quite cut it when compared to the Imperial Tea Court in Chinatown.

***

No trip to San Francisco would be complete without a walk in Golden Gate Park, including a stroll along the mile-and-a-half-long bridge that is the city's most prominent landmark. The Japanese Tea Garden is one of the most pleasant experiences offered by the park. It is tucked into a tranquil corner of the park where young woman in kimonos offered a passable tea service.

It was nothing truly special. No elaborate tea ceremonies. No fancy table settings. No high-back chairs. Just a simple covered area with a small tea shed, offering Jasmine, Oolong, Green and one or two other selections.

I had the Jasmine with a small saucer of cookies, including a fortune cookie that said something about a couple becoming close friends. It really didn't apply to me at the time but I kept it anyway. Maybe someday it would mean something but that afternoon, I was content to relax with my tea and read.

As I opened *The Maltese Falcon*, written by one of the city's most famous denizens, Dashiell Hammett, I recalled seeing a sign not too far from the Chinese tearoom I had visited earlier. It said that Miles Archer was murdered on this spot. Clearly someone was imbibing some kind of magic tea when City Hall allowed that sign to go up. After all, Archer was Sam Spade's partner and both were figments of Hammett's fertile imagination.

5 SOUTH AMERICA

"Under certain circumstances there are few hours in life more agreeable than the hour dedicated to the ceremony known as afternoon tea"

– Henry James in *The Portrait of a Lady*

A coca tea seller at the Inti Raymi festival in Peru.

Tea is maté in South America. It is especially common in countries like Uruguay and Argentina, but each country will have its own tea preference. Yerba maté is drunk in the south, coca tea in the high Andes further north. Tea travellers will recall the distinctive gourd tea cups specifically designed for drinking maté. Markets are brightened by kiosks selling painted, carved and leather-wrapped gourds. But if one is looking for afternoon tea, *thé anglais,* that is, one will usually be disappointed. It may be possible to get 'English' tea in the fancier hotels, but be advised that South America has its own tea traditions.

Peru's Coca Tea Craze
It helped build the Inca Empire and keeps tourists healthy today

Coca tea is to Cusco, Peru, what Earl Grey is to London. Well, not exactly, but it is equally ubiquitous in the land of llamas, condors and Lake Titicaca. Here, nestled in the breath-stealing peaks of the Andes a four-hour train ride from Machu Picchu, the 'lost city of the Incas', tourists can be seen sipping the hot greenish liquid throughout the day.

What has coca tea got to do with the short-lived Inca Empire? Partly it is about the herbal concoction's natural capacity to energize the imbiber. That was important for Inca soldiers and workers who literally moved mountains to build Machu Picchu, and many other phenomenal sites high in the mountainous regions of this South American country.

That July, Machu Picchu was named one of the seven 'new' wonders of the world and has been a United Nations World Heritage site since 1983. One could say that it is a testament to the quality of the coca tea that its builders must have consumed in great quantities.

The tea does several other things besides restoring energy levels, not the least of which is to act as a cure for altitude sickness. A few cups of this leafy brew and you're ready to climb Peru's highest peak, Mt. Huascarán, an extinct volcano that stretches to 6,768 meters or 22,205 feet. That's one reason why the Incas were able to thrive in the highlands almost half a millennium ago. It is also how tourists manage to see the remains of what they accomplished in less than two centuries from the 1300s to 1532 when Francisco Pizarro and his Spanish conquistadors showed up on horseback and began destroying the Inca empire stone by stone.

Weight-conscious travellers will be happy to learn that they can forget about those fancy California diets. This drink saps your body's desire for carbos almost instantly. In fact, the Inca workers who built Machu Picchu could go for days without food and still manage to transport thousands of stones to the site's 2,430-meter elevation almost 8,000 feet above sea level.

If you listen to some of the local tour guides, coca tea sounds like a cure-all drug, even capable of Viagra-like miracles. For that, though, the 219,759 foreign visitors who had been to Peru by May 2007 (up 13 per cent over 2006) may have to rely on another popular drink here, the pisco sour. At up to 45 per cent alcohol content, pisco can be a potent elixir, but it isn't designed for the heavy lifting required to erect monumental mountain citadels.

Old women wearing a variety of colourful traditional Peruvian hats sell coca leaves on the streets and in the markets of Cusco (population about 400,000) at one solé (about 30 cents) a bag. It can also be purchased along the spectacular sixty-eight-kilometre route through the Sacred Valley of the Incas heading towards Machu Picchu.

But don't get any ideas about buying your coca leaves *en masse* to boil down into pure cocaine. Yes, that is one of the properties of the leaves, but it takes a lot of them, it's illegal and no one wants an illicit drug cartel to accompany them on their travels along the Inca trail, a hiker's dream trek. Not to worry, though; drug lords won't be troubled if you sip a cuppa or two.

If you really need a shot of something different, try the local corn beer, chicha. Just watch for the red plastic bags hung outside hole in the wall shops anywhere in the Cusco region. Not so with coca tea. There are no coca tearooms. It is simply available everywhere and gringos are offered a cup at any hotel or hostel. You can even buy coca tea bags.

By the way, if you still have enough energy after climbing around Machu Picchu, head south to Lake Titicaca, one of the world's highest inland lakes. Take some coca leaves with you. It's several thousand feet higher than Cusco so you'll need a cup or two to clear your head way up there in the Andean clouds.

6 AFRICA

"There was a table set out under a tree in front of the house, and the March Hare and the Hatter were having tea at it: a Dormouse was sitting between them, fast asleep, and the other two were using it as a cushion, resting their elbows on it, and talking over its head. 'Very uncomfortable for the Dormouse,' thought Alice; 'only, as it's asleep, I suppose it doesn't mind'."

– *Alice in Wonderland,* Chapter 7 – A Mad Tea Party, by Lewis Carroll

Dollie clears the tea table at the Mount Nelson in Cape
Town, South Africa.

Those of us in the tea world who have enjoyed reading or seeing *The No. 1 Ladies Detective Agency* series will smile when recalling Precious Ramotswe drinking her bush tea. Adventurous tea travelers may have had it served to them while on safari in search of the Big Five in Kenya. Many other Africa countries have their own tea culture. North African countries like Morocco, for example, have their mint tea and so on. But the 'Dark Continent' also lives with the trappings of centuries of colonial rule. One of those trappings is high tea.

High Tea in Cape Town
From Robben Island prison to the colonial splendour of the Mount Nelson

A fine high tea is served at the Mount Nelson Hotel in downtown Cape Town, on the far west coast of South Africa. The reminder of British colonial times, with its massive pillared gate, welcomes mostly white patrons to stroll up a palm-lined road to the grand pink mistress of a bygone era vividly marked by apartheid.

Although that horrific racist regime ended in 1994, the Mount Nelson still reeks of the colonial past. A uniformed black man stands guard at the great sandstone gates that once barred entry to his kind. Still today there seems to be an unofficial colour barrier. Only blacks appear to be serving the almost all-white clientele, including those waiting table at The Lounge where high tea is served daily from 2 to 5 p.m.

A white woman welcomed me to the tearoom and I followed her past a large table overflowing with cakes and finger sandwiches, fruit cups and cheese trays. I stretched to get a fuller view while taking my place near the indoor patio overlooking the luscious gardens.

Two young black women in white chef's hats stood shyly at one end of a long wooden table that was decked out with all species of sweets and savouries. A lovely bouquet acted as the centerpiece. It was so tall that it almost touched one of the chandeliers above the carefully laid food trays.

My server was "Miss Dollie," a black woman in her late fifties who sported the kind of smile that made one want to hug her. It also revealed a special charm and keen awareness that only comes from years of serving tea people.

Miss Dollie paused to oblige three well-dressed white women by taking their picture as they sipped their bagged Dilmah Darjeeling and Earl Grey served in large white ceramic pots. A Thai company called Patra makes the fine ivory china and has been doing so since 1983.

A couple of mixed race are just leaving. The young children are restless and have been amusing themselves by dropping Warris of Sheffield silverware on the red tile floor. Miss Dollie is quick to remove the used china and scrub the table clean making it ready for the newly starched tablecloth. A black server rushes past with two handfuls of empty teapots.

"Experience one of the world's finest and most sumptuous afternoon teas," says the Mount Nelson brochure. But for all its boasting, there are no specials of the house, no scones or cakes exclusively designed to commemorate the long history of the pricey hotel.

Despite the brochure's claim of "a lavish spread of sandwiches, quiches, fresh berries, petit fours, chocolate éclairs and heavenly, decadent cakes," the food is traditional and quite ordinary tea fare. To redeem itself from such mediocrity, there is an endless quantity of it for the 140 rand plus 10 per cent tip (about $20). But it can't make up for the final insult: the tea is served in bags and the sugar in the paper tubes seen in South African hotels.

True that these packets are embossed with the words "The Mount Nelson" and sport the word "Sugar" in four languages. But they are still not what one expects in a quality tearoom. Would the nineteenth-century explorers Dr. David Livingstone and Mr. Henry Stanley have tolerated such effrontery? Would colonial imperialist and diamond mine magnate Cecil Rhodes have stood for bagged tea?

Certainly not, but then those men would not have allowed Miss Dollie to serve them either. That was a pleasure that in large part came with the release from prison of Nelson Mandela, signaling the death knell of apartheid.

***

An after-tea stroll around the extensive grounds of the Mount Nelson reveals lion's head statues, giant palms and ornate white streetlights. I craned my neck over the hedges in an attempt to see Robben Island in Table Bay, but it isn't visible from the quiet lawns of the Mount Nelson.

Earlier in the day I had visited the island where former South African president Mandela had been imprisoned. He and others were sent there for crimes against the apartheid government before that regime ended. The lavish old hotel, part of the Orient Express Hotels chain, still gives off that lingering sense of superiority and exclusion that marked that dark period of the country's history. Little Robben Island sits in the bay as a constant and vivid reminder of its horrors.

No doubt the Mount Nelson lives up to the brochure's billing as an "urban sanctuary" and an "oasis." Its high tea, however, could benefit from a similar revamping to what the buildings have recently received. It might also benefit from some cross-cultural revamping perhaps in the form of a Mandela or a Robben Island High Tea.

Tea at the Westcliff in Johannesburg
The view of the zoo is spectacular and the gooseberry tarts are...tart

Steve the cab driver's eyes widened as we pulled up to the main entrance of the Westcliff Hotel in Johannesburg, South Africa. "It will be 2,000 rand at least to stay here," he said in his strong South African accent. As he spoke I wondered what my tea was going to cost at this secluded enclave of former British colonialism.

"Try 3,000," I countered. The rate card later proved both of us wrong; it came closer to 3,500 rand or about $415. That's what it cost to stay in a "luxury room" at one of Joburg's most lavish hotels.

A parade of uniformed greeters and bag handlers and traffic controllers met us and Steve looked worried. His little red taxi was dwarfed by all the white Mercedes and dark blue deluxe Toyota vans.

"Where are you going?" asked one of the pill-box-wearing porters. Steve pointed to me, his white passenger and said something in Setswana, one of nine languages spoken here. The porter looked at me as if to check that I was the right colour, then let us pass.

I gave Steve an apologetic look and asked him to pull the car over to the front door so I could get the goods on the Westcliff from the concierge's desk.

Steve was anxious to leave the Westcliff, part of the esteemed Orient Express Hotels chain, and I didn't blame him. It seemed an unfriendly place to him and yet the hotel promotional literature suggested otherwise.

"The Westcliff estate has been created in the image of a Mediterranean village, with cobbled pathways, sparkling fountains and manicured cascading gardens," bragged the brochure.

"You can have it," Steve said. "I'll take a South African village any day."

***

"I want the tearoom," I told the concierge.

"That would be the Polo Lounge," he said, pointing up. Steve nodded and revved the Red Menace's engine. It was his way of giving the Westcliff the finger, I think.

We drove straight up a cobbled road to the tearoom. The Toyota shuttle buses take you to the top of the complex, but I jumped out half way and used an elevator.

The lounge sits high above the Joburg Zoo, a war museum and memorials to the dead killed in the world wars. It seemed a contradiction to have a zoo in a city like Joburg when visitors come to South Africa to go on safari where they can see the "Big Five" animals in the wild. Yet apparently many people visit the zoo as a starting point before taking on more adventurous outings in Kruger National Park and numerous other safari destinations.

A young white man greeted me at the tea lounge entrance. His nameplate said "Michael-Anthony" and he stuck out like a sore thumb in the middle of a team of black waiters. He didn't seem to mind being so conspicuous as he seated me at a window table for two. We groaned almost in unison when we saw that it was raining. Spits of it were jumping into the powder blue pool water below.

"It is a good view...when it isn't raining," Michael-Anthony said. "It's the start of winter in early May and it is usually dry. Grass and trees are beginning to go brown, so the rain will retard Nature's way for a few days," he went on. He seemed to think it was his duty to apologize for the weather or at least make an excuse for it.

The Westcliff tearoom is not nearly as lavish as the Mount Nelson, its sister in Cape Town. They are part of the same hotel chain and both offer the rich and famous the luxuries they have come to expect. So I was anticipating something quite special.

Eddy and Patrick, the waiters who were handling my side of the room, were busy lifting the large bell jars that protected the salmon, egg and cucumber finger sandwiches in the centre of the room. Michael-Anthony seemed to have disappeared for the moment.

I sat alone and quite far from these delicacies. On the other side of the lounge sat white families and well-dressed couples of various other colours. They all looked like they could afford to stay at the Westcliff. They looked Afrikaans to me, but they could have been anything. They also looked like they were used to the pampered treatment they were getting from the small army assisting them to have tea.

The dishware was nothing special at the Westcliff: Bauscher from Germany was more like crockery than china. The silverware is more impressive: Saint Andrea from France. The most impressive part of the table was the cup of whipped cream faking it as Devonshire clotted cream. Nuzzled close to it were four small jars of strawberry and apricot jam made by Hillcrest Berry Orchards in Stellenbosch.

The tea itself, Dilmah bagged English Breakfast, came in a metal pot that I promptly spilled on the until-then spotless white linen.

The spot spread out in a perfect brown circle and Eddy quickly rushed to my assistance. Or was it Patrick?

They managed to clean me up and I made for the sandwich tray, then it was over to the scones, then on to the tarts – raspberry, pecan, cream, gooseberry – and finally I stuffed a chocolate mousse cake with pistachio nuts whole into my mouth. I must have looked like a naughty school boy to the other tea diners…and to Michael-Anthony who had returned to his post and was staring at me disapprovingly.

I didn't care. I was going to eat and drink my fill. Did I have room for more? Perhaps a taste of the chocolate mousse topped with walnut crumbs and maybe a tiny cream puff. Maybe another bite of one of the three cakes I hadn't yet tasted. I did my best to act the boor. I was doing it for Steve, I told myself.

7 SOUTH PACIFIC

"Tea is not tea to the British unless it is poured into a cup. A cup, yes, but there is a class division centred on what precisely is meant by a cup…. The class division was made almost blatantly clear in World War II, when the commissioned officers took their tea in upper-class stained china in the officers' mess, while the rest of the army was issued with a mug that held half a litre of tea brewed coarsely in a bucket…. Britain could not have fought either of the two major wars of our century without tea."

– From the preface to *The Book of Tea* written by Anthony Burgess, Flammarion, Paris, 1992.

Tea in a Fijian village after indulging in some kava,
the South Pacific's other favourite beverage.

I was fortunate to spend three years in the South Pacific where tea, thanks to the long presence of the British, Dutch and other colonial powers, is part of the world's tea lands. Like other tea nations, those in the Asia-Pacific region have their own particularities when it comes to the serving of the beverage they inherited from their colonizers. Side by side with tea they also have another beverage, kava, which is much favoured by island men. In fact, one could say that kava rivals tea and has probably surpassed it in popularity, though some signs of tea's past glory are still in evidence.

Tea in Fiji
Afternoon sipping in an ancient Fijian village

I had planned to take tea at the Grand Pacific Hotel, probably the oldest and most celebrated hotel in Fiji at the time, maybe in the whole South Pacific. Queen Elizabeth and Prince Phillip had attended lavish balls here. The Royal couple dined overlooking the magical blue Pacific and no doubt sipped tea from exquisite GPH china.

Alas, when I arrived in the capital of Suva, the old white palace was boarded up and turning grey. The government of nearby Nauru had bought the famed landmark with intentions of restoring it to its former grandeur. But Nauru had run out of money and so had left the poor dear to rot.

Earlier I had enjoyed an afternoon tea at the luxurious Sheraton Royal Hotel on Denarau Island, a huge new tourist development near Nadi on the west coast of Fiji's Viti Levu Island. There they had served a uniquely Fijian mix of mini-lemon tarts, kiwi muffins and coconut scones. But I had my heart set on something extra-special.

Since my original tea plans had been scuppered by the Naurans, I widened my search by taking the twelve-minute Twin Otter flight from Nausori Airport, near Suva, to Ovalau. Here I hoped to have a tea experience that would more than make up for the disappointment of finding the GPH in such a decrepit state. But it would prove an elusive quarry.

* * *

Coming into the airport at Bureta was like landing in a cow pasture; a toy plane setting down on a toy-like airstrip. The narrow tarmac runway looked like a bike path from the air and seemed to end abruptly where the high grass and mangroves began at the other end.

Ovalau lies just to the east of Viti Levu where 70 per cent of the about 800,000 Fijians live. It was once destined for greatness as the location of the original capital of Levuka (population 3,745), but was eventually displaced by Suva (population 170,000).

It still has a lively history, of course, one that visitors can hear recounted by an old-timer in a unique eco-tourism offering. For $17.50, one can be invited into a Levukan home for tea and a chat (talanoa in the local language). But this was a pleasure that would have to wait. First it was off to visit Nukutocia, one of the twenty-three communities on the island.

"Bula vinaka, palagi," the children shouted as they ran along the dirt road leading into the village. Palagi means European but it seemed to be a catch-all phrase for white people. Semantics aside, the children seemed delighted to meet our party of Canadians here to see a Canadian-funded generator that would bring electricity to the village for the first time.

Tea would be served as part of an elaborate welcoming ceremony, but first we would partake of another social beverage, the notorious kava made from the crushed roots of the yaqona plant (pronounced yangona).

The uncrushed roots serve as sevu sevu, the gift customarily brought to the elders of a village. When crushed and mixed with water in a large, wooden, four-legged bowl, it forms a milky-grey liquid offered to visitors at all village ceremonies.

Once the dogs, cats and chickens had finished greeting us, we were escorted to an open-sided, dirt-floor building, not a traditional grass buré. Our shoes were left outside and our legs were tucked under us on hand-woven mats. We were warned earlier to be careful

143

not to point our toes in anyone's direction since that might give of-
fence.

The men of the village were dressed in colourful island shirts
and the traditional sulu, a skirt-like garment which palagi are advised
not to try wearing without an expert nearby to provide instruction
and thus save future embarrassment. As the ceremony began, the
women stayed in the background in their floral print skirts and
dresses.

After speeches accepted us into the village, the kava was
strained through thinly cut pandanus leaves, tested for appropriate
strength, then passed around in a half-coconut shell. First it was
served to the chiefs of the village. The, claps were heard as other
men indicated it was their turn in descending order of status.

The ceremony continued with two men placing a roast pig before us. It had been cooked in a lovo, an underground oven used to
steam meat and vegetables, and was wrapped in green banana leaves.
The smell of fresh pork drove the flies berserk. A woven basket of
breadfruit and papaya, coconut and plantain accompanied the pig.

As the kava circulated, the chief presented the coveted tabua, a
whale's tooth. The Fiji Museum in Suva has such a tooth on display
and with it came the gruesome story of a missionary who was canni-
balised because the tabua was sent ahead of him as a traditional con-
tract on his life. Happily, our tabua was given in peace and is a
unique Fijian way of honouring guests.

Finally, the women moved into the shack to present us with colourful pandanus leaf mats. They had been sitting patiently through
all the ceremonial speeches, each requiring an equally lengthy response from our party of foreign dignitaries. It was only when one of
the chiefs signalled to them to join in that they did so.

Finally, the tea I had been waiting for was about to be served. It
came in plain plastic mugs filled with milk and sugar as is the style
in the islands.

Back at Denarau Island, we had learned from Hari Punja, a tea
importer and possibly Fiji's richest man at the time, that the tea used
in Fiji was of low quality. Even his own Punja Tea brand was

plucked from middle- and low-growing areas of Sri Lankan plantations. "The best tea grows high up," he said. Hence the need for
milk and sugar in Fijian tea.

Plastic plates were placed on the mats, offering an abundance of
delicious sweet cakes and scones as well as cinnamon buns, a local
favourite. The pastry dough came from a mixture of yams, cane
sugar and coconut, and was baked in a communal oven.

Our tea finished, we were ready to leave Nukutocia. But first
we had to be 'released' by the chief as is the tradition. After a brief
speech and a reply, we got up stiff-legged from the ceremonial mats
and left the open-sided shack.

The women began to sing while the children ran about excitedly. Most of the men went back to their kava bowl. And I waved
and shouted a hesitant "mocé" (farewell), knowing that I would
never experience tea at the GPH the way I had in their tranquil village.

Tea in Samoa
Morning cuppa with a golfing monarch

The Marlon Brando Coffee Lounge at Aggie Grey's Hotel in Apia,
the capital of Samoa, no longer serves a proper tea. Instead, the visitor is confronted with a row of thirty jars of coffees from all over the
world. I would have to travel elsewhere for my cuppa. Elsewhere, as
it turned out, was at the official residence of His Highness Malietoa
Tamumafili II, then Samoa's Head of State.

I was quite sure that Marlon sipped neither tea nor guzzled coffee in the pleasant little corner lounge of this most famous of South
Pacific hotels. The wicker captain's chairs and tables, ship's lamps
and old photos create an inviting atmosphere for tea drinking.

However, I suspect Marlon and other stars like Gary Cooper and
William Holden gravitated to the bar to knock back Aggie's Specials
after a hot day's filming. Cooper, who stayed here while shooting
the 1953 film *Return to Paradise*, has a falé (bungalow) named after
him.

Out on Beach Road, Apia's main street, the Royal Samoa Police Band provided the coffee-drinking music. At precisely 7:50 a.m. each day, the band struck up a passable version of *Onward Christian Soldiers*. It seemed an appropriate choice for the morning flag-raising ritual in this sternly Christian country.

On the way to His Highness's official residence, driving deep into Apia (population 35,000), we passed a buzzing market. A boy and his mother sold fat, shiny, green plantain, the kind they bake with sugar and coconut. A hefty young woman sorted bundles of thinly cut pandanus leaves to be used as strainers for coconut milk. An old woman, cigarette dangling from her lips, worked at weaving a traditional fine mat. Middle-aged men played a game with bright blue and yellow disks.

Bright yellow, pink and blue home-made busses passed us along the way to the comparatively modest home of His Highness. When he became Head of State for life at independence in 1962, he had lived at Vailima, the lavish estate built by writer Robert Louis Stevenson in the 1890s. But he had to vacate the home of Tusitala (Teller of Tales) as Samoans named the author of *Treasure Island*, *Kidnapped* and other boy's adventure stories.

Some government official had decided that Vailima should be converted to a museum which includes RLS's silver tea set. Unfortunately there was no longer room to house the island nation's head of state.

When we arrived, Malietoa, then 84, was wearing a brown sports jacket and light brown lavalava, the traditional Samoan skirt worn by men. He held my right arm as we posed for photos, then walked me over to a couch where we had morning tea at a marble-topped table. Like old men tend to do, he shuffled along in his brown slippers.

The tea came with a tray of white-bread finger sandwiches (cucumber) and some delicious baked goods, both sweet and savoury. Probably the best tea I would have in Samoa, it was served by a man in white uniform on an unpretentious set of Yamanto china.

***

On the other side of Upolu, the main island, I had taken tea at Sinalei Reef Resort, which is dedicated to fa'a Samoa or traditional Samoan ways. I had eaten their delicious pineapple meringue pie and banana strudel. But I had found only one other possible tea place in Apia and that was the Black Coffee Café.

The name didn't hold out much hope, but once inside the breezy, open space I spotted a row of tea canisters marked Twining's English Breakfast, "Ceylon Supreme." Healtheier's camomile and even blackcurrant were also available.

Tea was placed on my black and white tapa-covered table along with four-inch-across fruit scones and mini-beer jugs of raspberry jam and butter. I also ordered a tall, milkshake-thick blend of tropical juices and a copy of the *Samoan Observer.*

***

As we sipped tea with His Highness, he rambled through a mental list of Canadian reference points, clapping as he struck each one off the list, whispering them aloud as he did so. Friendly interjections were pointless; His Highness was hard of hearing. When he finished his list, he moved on to his days as a student in New Zealand. He gestured to his necktie which was adorned with a yellow kiwi bird, one of New Zealand's national symbols.

Finally, having run out of semi-official niceties, he turned to me and asked the hard-ball question: "Do you play golf?" Previous visitors had briefed me that His Highness was a golf enthusiast who asked all male visitors the same question.

"Yes, I play golf, Your Highness," I replied. "In fact, my father was a golf teacher." That prompted a round of hand claps similar to those we had seen old men make when they wanted more kava, the slightly intoxicating social drink preferred by men in the islands. South Pacific women seem to prefer low-quality tea with lots of milk and sugar. Then a huge smile beamed across the still handsome face.

"You will golf with me tomorrow, yes?" he said. It was more of a command than a question. I imagined myself in long pants and heavy socks, sweating through four hours of 35C heat when I could be sipping tea and sucking back coconut juice on the beach at Palolo Deep, the popular snorkelling area not far from Aggies.

"I'm actually a terrible golfer," I backtracked, spilling tea, "a duffer really." I hadn't held a club in twenty years and when I did play it was with an unfixable slice that kept me in bad temper and in the rough looking for my ball much of the game. "I'd have to claim the maximum handicap," I said, searching for any excuse.

"Oh, that's fine. I hope you don't mind playing with a bunch of old men," His Highness went on. "I'm sure we won't take too much of your Canadian money! More tea?" He was having a good chuckle and I was feeling doomed.

"I have a golf bag for you," he clapped in delight. "We will arrange it for after lunch. Say about 1:30 p.m." I was trapped. You don't say no to someone whose first name is Your Highness.

Resolved to my fate, I returned to Aggie's. Not long after that, I learned that the deputy head of state had just died. Suddenly, I realized that I had been rescued. His Highness would have to cancel his Wednesday afternoon golf game to attend the state funeral that was no doubt being arranged. I was off the hook!

A call to one of His Highness's assistants confirmed that he would indeed need to cancel. Profuse apologies. I strained to hide my relief, for I felt sure that I would have embarrassed myself and my country on the links.

I thought of playfully remarking that I would require a rain check, but wisely decided to keep quiet as I made my way past the Marlon Brando Coffee Lounge and into the bar for a double Aggie's Special.

Tea in Tonga
Taking tea with difficulty in a dieting Pacific kingdom

There were roadside weigh stations in Tonga when I visited, but they were not for freight-hauling trucks and other commercial vehicles. They were for people registered in the fourth annual weight-loss competition, probably the only such contest anywhere in the world. It did not bode well for hungry tea seekers like me.

This is the last of the Polynesian monarchies and King Taufa'ahau Tupou IV was keen that his subjects should shed some kilos. Hence, the weigh stations and hence the unlikelihood that afternoon tea here might be available. It seemed it might be more taboo than tapu (Tongan for sacred). Royal decree had put the kibosh on any over-indulging in sweet taro bread laced with coconut milk and other fattening island fare.

The king was leading by example and was apparently thinning out nicely as he prepared to celebrate his eightieth birthday that July 5. On "Royal diet" days, a motorcycle escort – lights flashing, sirens screaming – flanked his motorcade driving to and from the "Royal workout." That occurred regularly on Wednesdays and Fridays. Royal subjects were encouraged to follow His Majesty's lead.

There are many obviously heavy eaters among the 100,000 Tongans living on about fifty of the one hundred and seventy islands sprinkled over 700,000 square kilometres of Pacific Ocean. So the weight-loss plan is undoubtedly a good thing for these so-called Friendly Islands.

Captain James Cook dubbed them that in 1777. Ironically, he dropped anchor here to water and wood his vessel despite rumours that the less than friendly islanders intended to eat him. Regrettably, the king's diet promised to be an unfriendly act aimed at tea travellers as well.

Tongans are deservedly famous, not for their tea, but for their feasts. Even the smallest villages will prepare mammoth quantities of piglets cooked to a dark brown, whole chickens wrapped in cellophane and dripping grease, plates of fried fish and canned corned beef, mounds of taro and breadfruit, carrots and other vegetables. Add to that immense mountain of food, bowls of taro leaves boiled in coconut milk, plastic containers filled with plantain cooked in a sweet syrup, sweet and sour beef, potato salad, pineapple and watermelon in heaping piles. It was a feast fit for Gulliver.

Tea is still drunk here, of course, but it's either a private affair or a very public one reserved for honoured visitors and guests attending special ceremonies like the king's birthday. And even then it might not be offered.

During a morning audience with the king, tea would not necessarily be served. Instead, it could be substituted with a glass of bubbly and a bowl of cheese puffs or Tongan peanuts with Cadbury chocolates as a sweet.

A less auspicious tea occasion might still be on offer at Talamahu Market in the capital city of Nuku'alofa (place of love). There one can feast one's eyes on the many exotic fruits and vegetables grown in the islands. But tea will likely be served in a Styrofoam cup at one of the small food booths around the outer edge of the market. A huge block of sticky coconut bread will invariably accompany it.

As you sip standing protected from the tropical sun, you might see an old woman offering raw peanuts still on the branch. An old man might have just hacked open a fresh young coconut to suck it dry of its milky contents. Mothers and daughters might be selling green oranges, pineapples, giant taro roots and fat cooking bananas.

Of course you can get tea at the hotels and restaurants in Nuku'alofa (population 20,000), but with no fanfare. The best restaurant in town is the German-run Seaview where you can undoubtedly get a good cuppa after a meal of something fresh-caught or some imported beef. But for the most part it is the same sweet, milky bag tea that is offered throughout the South Pacific islands.

At the International Dateline Hotel, Nuku'alofa's finest, I had such a tea one evening while watching an old-timers' band sit around the dining lounge sipping kava, the dish-watery liquid made from a local root that is the favoured beverage throughout the islands.

After drinking their fill, two wrinkle-faced old fellows plunked their ukuleles, one of them specially crafted by a ukulele maker in the far-off Cook Islands. Another strummed a sea-water-stained old guitar while a fourth throttled a jaded violin. Several bottles of wine made the rounds to replace the kava and the music got better as the night wore on.

The next day I visited the one hundred and thirty-two-year-old Tupou Boy's College, Tonga's oldest. No slouch in the tea department, the school principal ordered tea served on silver with great plates of white-bread egg sandwiches and tasty biscuits.

A young woman dressed in black brought the tea. She, not the tea, was wrapped in a large handmade pandanus leaf mat. This is traditional dress in Tonga and many people wear mats daily as a sign of respect. While indulging in these treats I was serenaded by a boy's choir singing *The Lion Sleeps Tonight* and the college brass band played some fine marching tunes.

As I finished my tea, a female dancer covered in mats, her skin plastered with coconut oil, contorted her body with the slow, wavy moves of a traditional dance called the lakalaka. I would see similar dancing during a feast at the Dateline later in the week followed by a virtuoso performance on a tiny electric ukulele. The dancer's body was clearly in no need of the king's diet...yet.

Of course, most Tongans would want to heed the admonitions in the *Tongan Chronicle* to cut down on the starch and eat your vegetables. The weekly newspaper was clearly on side with the king's weight loss campaign.

"Decide the amount of food on your plate and do not have a second helping," it advised. But then again most Tongans don't seem very worried about size. After all, sitting next to a large Tongan, nicely wrapped up in a thick rug, is a comfort of a different kind.

All the Tongan feasting makes a standard Victorian cream tea in the afternoon seem like a dieter's delight. But alas you will not find one of those in Tonga. Perhaps someone will see fit to start a tearoom in the Place of Love some day. Of course, they would have to skip those years that are devoted to the king's weight-loss program!

Tea with a Maori Queen
Celebrating the coronation of Dame Te Ata on the royal marae

I arrived at Turangawaewae Marae on the fourth day of a grand ceremony marking the thirty-second anniversary of the Maori Queen's coronation. I had long hoped for a chance to take tea with a queen. Getting an invitation to a Buckingham Palace tea was never in the cards. Now it looked like it might happen with royalty of another kind.

Te Arikinui Dame Te Atairangikaahu – Dame Te Ata for those with understandably reticent tongues – was crowned in 1966 at the death of her father, the fifth Maori king, Koroki Mahuta. And I was with a party of diplomats that had been invited to join in the royal celebration.

The first king, Pootatau Te Wherowhero, ascended to the throne in 1858. He wore a full-facial tattoo (moko mokai), a heavy stone earring and carried a meré (flat stone club). He was a scary-looking dude, dressed and made-up partly to counter the equally scary looking image of Queen Victoria or at least to assist in negotiations with the old British queen's emissaries.

The Maori did not give up their land without a fight. In fact, the Maori wars in the nineteenth century were a bloody affair that showed they were not easily intimidated by such ephemeral notions as royalty. Anyway, figuring that anyone could invent their own king and queen, that's what they did, thank you very much.

Dame Te Ata belongs to the Tainui tribe and it is one of the better endowed, according to the 1997 annual report of the Tainui Maaori Trust Board and Waikato Raupatu Lands Trust. Waikato is the river valley where the Tainui settled after coming to New Zealand by canoe (waka). Rauputa refers to a specific land area.

***

I arrived via Ngaruawahia, a village slightly northeast of Hamilton, New Zealand's largest inland city, and was soon given a royal welcome to the royal gathering place. At 10:30 a.m. I was greeted by a waiting delegation from the queen led by the Honourable Koro Tainui Wetere. I later learned that he was the Maori affairs minister in New Zealand's Labour government from 1984-1990.

Koro escorted me through the gates of the marae, understandably one of the most elaborately carved and painted sacred places in Maoridom, and up the path towards a waiting formation of Maori men. They proceeded with the usual challenge (haka) and what a challenge it was! I had been through a similar exercise at Government House in Wellington, New Zealand, but somehow this setting seemed much more culturally appropriate.

A colourful dart was laid between our party and the near-naked Maori warriors. We were being asked whether we came in peace or war in this wonderful ceremonial way, but it meant much more being in the Maori queen's home territory.

Koro picked up the dart and gave it to me. It was a beauty, carefully carved and stained, then painted black and white with small paua (abalone) buttons inset in the wood.

Once we had faced the challenge, a choir of fifty elderly women dressed in black, stood to sing a welcoming song (waiata) for us. Each of them waved a garland of green silver fern, a symbol of Aotearoa. (The Maori name for New Zealand means 'Land of the Long White Cloud'.) It was a moving and humbling scene observed by several hundred people.

Our party joined Dame Te Ata and her husband Whatamoano (pronounced fatta moe ana) on the platform at the entrance to Mahinarangi, the whare tupuna (ancestral house) where dignitaries are received. She met us with the usual broad smile I'd seen in photos and I was invited to sit by her side. It was sunny one minute and rainy the next, so she was bundled up in a warm afghan.

The Maori elders said their welcomes, the women sang after each man spoke, then one of the diplomats spoke on behalf of the visiting party. She thanked them for flying her country's flag and gestured to it flapping steadily at the far end of the performing area.

Some fabulous Maori dancing began the royal ceremony and the master of ceremonies guided us through every step of the dancing, explaining the significance of costume designs in a quiet whisper and noting the origin of each group of dancers. Whenever a particular dance move struck him as of high quality, he gasped in delight. Dame Te Ata and Whatamoana did the same, leaning over to tell us why a given haka was important to the Maori and what it signified historically.

The queen said the haka was "a good way to get rid of all your frustrations," a kind of stress reliever. "They get quite wound up whenever the haka is directed at government," she said, giving me the elbow and giggling. I liked her. She had no shortage of spunk and this queen knew how to speak truth to power; you dance it in their faces.

We broke for tea served on a silver service with scones, muffins and cakes with pink icing. Inside Mahinarangi I found a magnificent collection of Maori artifacts – canes, carvings, merés, spears, paddles, sculptures and other objects. In the centre was a metal bird that had been repatriated from Te Papa, New Zealand's national museum. The bird came to the shores of Aotearoa with the first Tainui waka. Above it sat a large carved throne for the queen.

The winners of the dancing competition got to perform for Dame Te Ata and her guests. At one point, the dancers – women in black, white and red tops and straw skirts, men bare-chested with grass skirts and black shorts – were set against a stunning Waikato Valley rainbow.

At 1 p.m. we broke for a quick tour of the facilities, including a makeshift dormitory, a clinic that had already treated six rugby injuries that day, and the great dining hall called Kimiora that was opened in 1974 by Queen Elizabeth II. The hall's walls were covered in carvings depicting the history of the Maori queen's ancestors.

Lunch followed in the dining room at Turongo House, the queen's official residence. I was seated across from Koro Wetere and beside the leader of the Maori Party, an attractive thirty-something woman trying to hide a flu-ridden red nose.

The meal began with smoked eel, fat Bluff oysters (Dame Te Ata hooked a huge one and giggled as she set it down on her plate), Havelock mussels on the half-shell with an orange-coloured sauce, and a seaweed concoction that I didn't dare risk tasting.

Dame Te Ata frowned in disapproval, saying that I would never find such a delicacy in any restaurant. I also passed on the kina, the roe of sea urchins. This time the Maori Party leader uttered the admonition. "A Maori delicacy," she said through her sniffles.

During the main course – fish with a green sauce, capsicum (bell peppers) and lettuce salad with kumara (Maori for sweet potato) – the politician told me her party is part of the Alliance Party, a left-of-centre coalition. Labour Party leader Helen Clark would have to come to her senses and form a coalition with the Alliance to win the 1999 elections, she said, as if I might be chatting with Helen sometime soon. (As it turned out Clark won the election and sat for three terms as prime minister.)

I'm getting better at detecting when I'm being used by a politician. I have my antennae high now. She wanted something. Was it access to someone in the diplomatic corps back in Wellington? Was it her intention to push the native land claims agenda? Maybe, maybe not.

After dessert – feijoa crumble with ice cream – I asked her and Koro if they had seen *Primary Colours*, the John Travolta movie about President Bill Clinton's exploits and sexploits. They seemed unaware of it. I explained what it was about and they rather sheepishly ducked any further discussion. Politicians!

We took another cup of tea and some photographs with Dame Te Ata and it was time to leave. Of course, you don't just walk out of the queen's marae with a short thank you and good-bye. Oh no! When our party stepped outside, the large gathering parted to let us through and near the performing area stood the MC at a microphone.

He launched into a song in Maori that he had composed in honour of our party's visit to the royal marae. Some of the performers formed a choir. He ended with a few words of French, and as he did so, I silently saluted Dame Te Ata a final time. This was a royal tea for me to remember.

Postscript
A tealess festival at Dame Te Ata's marae

The Aotearoa Traditional Maori Performing Arts Festival gave me a second opportunity to join the Maori queen on Turangawaewae marae. This time tea was not really on the menu but the experience was memorable just the same.

The festival has been going since 1972 and this was the second time it had been held on Dame Te Ata's marae. I got invited because two aboriginal dance groups from Canada were performing during the three-day event.

As usual, the American ambassador took the lion's share of attention during the opening ceremonies. The kuia (pronounced queeia), powerful elderly women in Maori communities, even added a little Louis Armstrong coda to the end of their waiata, much to the American's delight.

There was more subdued, New-Zealand-style fanfare for Governor General alongside Sir Michael and Lady Hardie Boys when they arrived on the marae. The Maori were flying high above any official protocol on this occasion. In fact it was a breach of diplomatic protocol for the American to be put ahead of the Malaysian head of the diplomatic group that was also in attendance. But the Tainui Trust wasn't obliged to observe such pakeha (white or European) rules.

I wandered over to the porch of the whare where dignitaries were seated to hear the speeches – the many, many speeches in Maori – from representatives of the tengata whenua (indigenous peoples) and the manuhiri (non-Maori visitors). The American sat in the front row and the elders paid deference, making more than passing references to "America."

The two highlights of the day were the haka that took place before the official opening. Two of the Maori leaders appeared to be taking the haka more seriously than it was meant to be during a ceremonial performance. They were into doing battle. Merés flashed, clubs swirled. It was quite a spectacle and it lasted about thirty minutes.

I overheard Whatamoana, the queen's spouse, saying that it was a genuine grudge match between the two leaders. I had become used to ceremonial haka, so this was a particular treat. It gave me some idea of how truly ferocious and threatening the ritual can be.

When they finished sparring and the opening ceremony had come to and end, three waka or war canoes came up the Waikato River. Each had about forty warriors paddling in full battle formation and they did it up well. If it was one hundred and forty years ago and you saw one of these babies coming at you, you'd be afraid!

When I turned to the queen to say how awed I was by the sight of the waka, she asked, "Can you imagine them wearing life jackets?!" She obviously couldn't and was alluding to a suggestion that they should be forced to do so. A young man had died at New Year's and it had stirred up the debate about life jackets.

Tea would be served soon, but not before I got immense amusement out of watching Lady Hardie Boys, in her funny little straw hat, join the kuia in singing several waiata. She seemed to know all the words. I was impressed and joked with her later that she should give us all lessons. Maybe at the next afternoon tea party at Government House?

Tea by the Sea Down Under
Along the famed Shipwreck Coast one might find the best
scone in Oz

I had almost given up hope of finding a memorable Australian tearoom when I got to Airey's Inlet, a tiny village overlooking the
Southern Ocean along Australia's Great Ocean Road. Not far up the
coast, the Twelve Apostles stick their craggy limestone heads out of
the choppy sea. They and other natural wonders at the bottom of the
world make the coastal views stunningly beautiful. But I certainly
did not anticipate finding any tearooms. A pub or ten maybe, but tearooms in rough and ready Aussie?

I had been reading Frank Hardy's 1962 novel, *Power Without
Glory*, in which Cummin's Tearoom in Melbourne plays a signifi-
cant role as the main venue for rags-to-riches gangster John West's
horse-betting operations. It made me wonder if all Australian tearooms were once fronts for some illegal activity and thus closed
down years ago.

I also realized that, as a former penal colony, many of the early
inhabitants might have craved something stronger than tea in their
leisure hours. Cultural icons like the bush scout and larrikin (rogue)
Ned Kelly probably didn't reach for the teapot first thing in the
morning.

Nor was a fine English tearoom the likely first choice of tough-
but-kind horsemen like the *Man from Snowy River* made famous
through Australian bush poet Banjo Paterson's 1890 poem, and then
a television series and several films.

A visit to Oz teaches you that the locals have a definitive taste
for their pot, middie or schooner of Touhey's Old, Foster's Lager or
a Victoria Bitter (which isn't really a bitter at all). Many Aussies
also have a well-developed palate for the myriad local wines that
line the shelves of 'Bottle Shops' on virtually every street corner.

Coffee seems to have become another national favourite. Spend
a Saturday strolling the distinctly cosmopolitan Lygon Street in
Melbourne and you'll smell what I mean. And the Australians won't

accept just any coffee. They are as finicky as tea drinkers. Will that be a short or long black (straight espresso), a flat white (latte in a cup, although some Australians will argue forever that it's not!), a latte (in a glass), a cappuccino, or a macchiato?

But surely tea, the quintessential British hot beverage, played a major role in the colonization of this great subcontinent, you say. Oh, the tourist shops are full of something called Outback Tea, an herbal mix of indigenous origins. And they do grow tea in Queensland, not to mention being geographically near tea-growing nations like Indonesia, Malaysia and other former colonies.

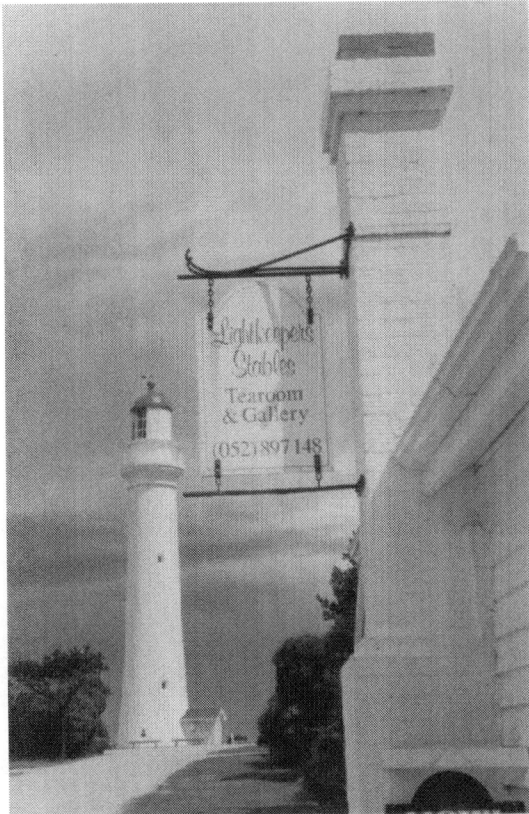

The Lighthouse Tearoom at Airey's
Inlet on Australia's shipwreck coast.

Then again, there always seems to be some sort of secessionist threat down under. On one of my tea visits there was a budding movement here to withdraw from the Commonwealth, dump Queenie and form a republic. Aussie seems, after all, to be more akin to the United States in some ways, than to the mother country.

Perhaps it was a sign of crumbling empire when British tea merchant Sam Twining, heir to the Twining tea empire, gave Australians a tea-making lesson during a visit to Melbourne in October 1995. Had he thought they'd forgotten? Was it a sign that the most southerly former colony in the British Empire was dismissing tea along with the monarchy?

Of course, I could have taken tea at any number of places in Melbourne. But after much research the only vestige of authentic tearoom lore seemed to be the Hopetown Tearooms in the Victorian splendour of the Block Arcade. There I sipped a loose Darjeeling in the usual metal pot with a not-so-usual pumpkin scone, jam, and whipped cream.

The menu suggested that tea drinkers "take your mind back to the late 19th century," when a Lady Hopetown founded the tearoom in 1892 as head of the Victorian Ladies Work Association. It still had the ambience of a charity bake sale about it and was long past its glory days when I visited, I'm afraid.

And so it was that my search for an Australian tearoom took me to the Great Ocean Road, a spectacular, though often narrow, highway that weaves along the coast eventually to arrive at Adelaide. Scenery galore, yes, but I was clearly a long way from enjoying any real Devonshire or Cornish cream along the shipwreck coast...or was I?

I found what I was looking for about fifty kilometres southwest of Geelong, Victoria's second city (one hundred and fifty kilometres from Melbourne). It was called the Lighthouse Stables Tearoom and Gallery after the magnificent 1892 vintage lighthouse that marks its location.

The three-table Lighthouse Tearoom – yes, I said 'three' – and a cramped art and pottery gallery are housed in what used to be the lighthouse keeper's stables. That was before the storybook lighthouse was automated in 1919. The picnic tables outside were surrounded by a flower garden and Jacaranda trees were starting to bloom into giant purple bouquets.

Below the tearoom and the lighthouse a gaggle of school children searched the craggy shore for shells. The sweet smell of white and mauve wildflowers was everywhere and silver-backed seabirds flapped about like drunken sunbathers.

Back at the Lighthouse Tearoom, I ordered a pot of Sri Lankan called Coombs from among seven others including a wild cherry tisane. While warming a fresh scone, Lois Jackman explained that they had opened in 1993 and were doing quite well thanks to international tea travellers like myself.

The gallery displayed works by local artists, mostly paintings of the awe-inspiring coastline, especially Split Point and the stunning Eagle Rock poking out of Loutit Bay on the Bass Strait. There were also shells on sale and ceramic ware as well as locally produced honey, condiments and preserves.

I chose Gentle Annie's blackberry jam to go with my scone and a cream that seemed close to the Devonshire variety on offer at several bed and breakfasts up and down the coast. I later learned that King Island off Tasmania produces excellent clotted cream and wondered why the locals weren't promoting a King Island Cream Tea.

The tea was served loose in plain white porcelain with a side pot of hot water, a strainer with matching holder, milk in a creamer and sugar in a bowl. The scone came in a small basket wrapped in a cloth napkin to keep it warm and was among the best I've ever eaten.

I would find other tearooms during my visits to Australia. There would be the Boston Tearoom in Brisbane, with its "psychic readings," and the Kookaburra Queen, a restored paddle-wheeler luring tourists to take a very bad tea while suffering through an unimaginative Brisbane River tour. And there was the odd teashop in coffee-stained Sydney, most of them too expensive for even my taste.

For the money, authenticity and view, the Lighthouse Tearoom at Airey's Inlet was as good as they come down under.

Tea at the Great Barrier Reef
Ulysses butterflies, dainty sea horses and the tea delights of the Daintree Rainforest

"You picked a fine time to leave me, Lucille" rattled from the cheap speakers of the tourist bus that brought me from Cairns (pronounced Cans by the locals) to Port Douglas and the tea country of Far North Queensland in Australia.

It wasn't the music I had expected to hear on entering Australia's answer to Fiji or Bali. Here is where "reef meets rainforest," as the television tourism ads put it. Somehow Lucille did not fit the images that fluttered through my imagination: delicate electric blue Ulysses butterflies, colourful seahorses in an undersea garden of coral, or the cane sugar crops swaying in the warm tropical breeze.

But then neither did the Daintree Tea Company fit my image of a plantation that grows and processes "full-bodied, unblended Australian tea which captures the aromas" of the surrounding Daintree Rainforest. In fact, I didn't have an image of a rainforest tea estate at all when I stopped at the Nicholas family operation near Cape Tribulation off the 2,300-kilometre Great Barrier Reef.

To my pleasant surprise they had been growing "naturally low in caffeine" and "free from tannic acid" tea since 1978. But they weren't the first to do so. The four Cutten brothers had that honour.

The brothers came to Queensland from England in the 1880s to set up the first tea plantation at nearby Mission Beach. They hired a former Ceylon tea planter to teach them the basics and the crops thrived. For some reason, the brothers abandoned rainforest tea and switched to coffee, eventually selling it all over Australia. About a hundred years later the Nicholas family succeeded where the Cuttens had failed.

The Cubbagudta plantation (it means rainy place in the language of the Kuku Yulangi aboriginal people) is nestled into the Daintree wilderness where the heavy rainfall (about 4,000 millimetres a year) combines with the granite alluvial red soils to allow the Nicholas family to grow tea free from insecticides and fungicides.

They had used a painting of the endangered cassowary, Australia's second largest flightless bird, on the packages of their "environmentally friendly tea." And it was an appropriate image for it is the cassowary that ensures the survival of the rainforest through a unique 'beak to bum' ecological system. They and the equally unique combination of weather and soil ensure that the tea crop will flourish.

The tea is produced in twenty-four hours assuring ultimate freshness for the local markets it mainly supplies. Although few of Port's numerous cafes, restaurants and tearooms served the unique brand, I was able to buy loose and bagged varieties at local tourist shops.

When I asked for it at the exclusive Sheraton Mirage resort, tucked between a strip of rainforest and stunning Four Mile Beach, they offered only Twining brand teas at their daily high tea served in the Daintree Lounge.

The framed poster at one lounge entrance displayed a group of happy tea drinkers and dancers and it announced "High Tea" as one of the "Daintree Delights." Two great silver samovars sat at the other entrance. A wooden "Cigar Corner" humidor was no doubt meant for clients of another kind of Daintree Delight offered later in the day.

Surrounding me were several wrought-iron sculptures of egrets much like the live ones seen standing one-footed on the mud flats of Cairns at twilight. A photo exhibit by local artist Ric J. Steininger included shots of Uluru (Ayer's Rock), and several paintings, one of a flame tree set in Fiji, brought more colour to the tea scene.

As I sat down, the table was set with silverware by Saint Andrea and "Kutani Crane" by Wedgewood. The silver tea service was "Beard of Montreux" from Switzerland. One of two servers wheeled over a large wooden trolley its glass display case bulging with tea treats.

While my Prince of Wales loose tea was being poured, a man whisked past to place a small vase of freshly arranged purple and white orchids in front of me. This was certainly a surprising slice of tea culture to find in the Australian rainforest wilderness!

We started with a selection of savouries: smoked salmon (heaps of it) stuffed into triangular sandwiches, minced chicken and chili on cucumber slices garnished by a tiny mint leaf, ham with papaya chutney on melba with thyme rolled into the ham, beef with *jus d'onion* (onion relish) on pumpernickel set off by thin lines of mustard. Each had a distinct set of flavours.

The scones were served with whipped, not clotted, cream and a choice of blackberry, apricot and strawberry jams. But it was the pastries that overwhelmed me. They were the highlight no doubt thanks to the careful supervision of the hotel's French general manager Michel Cottray.

Chocolate mud cake was the centrepiece with its large flanges of chocolate adorning the top layer. The apricot strudel was made with the lightest of *milles feuilles* pastry. Macadamia nut cake was appropriate given that Queensland is the original home of the nut grown on the nearby Atherton Tablelands.

The coconut slices with lightly toasted almonds and delicate glazing were also suitable tropical fare grown in the region. Also on offer were hazelnut-chocolate torte, carrot cake, lemon sponge cake and honey-glazed whole strawberries as sweet as can be. It was a feast by any tearoom standards, wilderness or no.

I would have tea again that week. Once on the Waveslicer roaring out to a multi-levelled reef playground called Quicksilver. I would also imbibe again in Port at the town's enjoyable Sunday Markets. It was there that I purchased a used copy of *The Republic of Tea Book of Tea & Herbs*, a reminder that Aussie hadn't totally forgotten its tea roots even if it wasn't a republic.

Still, on reflection the high tea at the Sheraton for $15 might have been the only true tea bargain among Port's growing expanse of hotels, cafes, bars, tour operators, car and video rental stores, opal shops and aboriginal art galleries. It was indeed a 'delight' that could only be enhanced by serving the Daintree Tea Company brand.

Tasmanian Tea
Of devils and convicts and billy tea by the bucketful

There are devils in Tasmania and wombats and there used to be Tasmanian tigers. Heck, you can even visit the "Platypus capital of the world" in this former penal colony at the deep south end of the earth. And tea is best taken in the wild, too.

That's just what I did at Bonorong Wildlife Park, a short drive from the village of Tea Tree and about thirty kilometres from Hobart, the capital of what *Conde Nast Traveler* declared the "world's best temperate island."

The park is on the road to historic Richmond where the first 'gaol' was constructed in the 1820s. Convicts built the oldest bridge in Australia there in 1823 and the town boasts the oldest Catholic Church in Aussie as well.

Bonorong provides a natural setting for its inhabitants, and the main attractions tend to be the koalas, not native to the island, and Tasmanian Devils. Watching the young park attendant feed rabbit carcasses to devils almost put me off my tea. Fortunately, we moved on to two baby wombats that resembled a pair of miniature Sherman tanks.

Then it was over to the echidnas. Ugly-cute like many other Australian animals, these little critters looked akin to Volkswagen Beetles and waddled like porcupines. After that it was Erica the emu with her gorgeous orange eyes. Peacocks strutted and honked as I fed wallabies and kangaroos, their pouches bursting with young.

Bonorong means "native companion" in the local Aborigine dialect. And I took advantage of the park's open concept to get as close to the quolls, pademelons and possums as I could, even coaxing two cockatoos to say "Hello, Cookie."

By the time I got to the Bush Tucker Shed Café, I was good and ready for a hearty outdoor tea. It's called billy tea in 'Tassie' and the rest of outback 'Oz' and it comes with a healthy portion of "bush damper" or flat bread instead of scones. It is brewed in a tin can usually over an open fire. A handful of tea – the outback variety might well contain a few eucalyptus twigs – is tossed in and the concoction is boiled until it's nice and dark.

The damper is made in a pan and comes in large round loaves. They are sometimes a little burnt around the crust due to the open fire, but soft and delicious inside. Two huge portions arrived on a platter with my tea. Three small bowls contained "lashings" of local berry jam, apple butter and honey.

Tasmania, although cooler than the rest of Australia, is honeybee heaven in the spring and summer. Near Launceston, the island's second largest city, is Bridestowe, the largest lavender farm in the region. And all through the Northern Midlands, right across to Devenport, white poppies grow, row upon row.

Of course, the poppy gardens weren't put there simply for the joy of bees and honey with afternoon tea. Legal pharmaceutical heroin had become an important export and a key player in the island economy. 'Keep out' signs warded off any misguided drug fiends.

Turning back to my table I noticed another white substance: a tea drinker's drug in the form of a huge dollop of cream languishing in its own large bowl. I hoped it might be clotted cream from nearby King Island, where the cheeses are the most famous in Australia. But alas, it was whipped cream.

I shouldn't have been too surprised. At $6.50 for the bush damper and billy tea, I suppose asking for clotted cream was out of the question. It isn't usually part of tea-drinking habits anywhere in the Asia-South Pacific region. Even the "Devonshire teas" offered at farms throughout the dry grazing land of the Midlands will not come with such cream.

**

Earlier, in Richmond, I visited The Tea Chest, a small tea and coffee shop near the famous jail and bridge. The clerk had no cream to offer either, but she did give me several sachets of a local Australian Irish Breakfast tea called Madura that was quite palatable. London and Harrogate teas seemed to crowd her shelves in an all-out battle not to be pushed into oblivion by the growing numbers of 'flavoured' coffees.

Richmond jail is, of course, where Australian novelist Bryce Courtenay learned about Ikey Solomon, the model for Dickens's Fagin in *Oliver Twist*. The incorrigible Solomon, who was a key figure in Courtenay's *The Potato Factory*, was an inmate there and in other jails around the notorious penal subcontinent.

Earlier still, I had indulged in a tea at Felon's Restaurant at historic Port Arthur, the bloodiest penal colony in Australia. Tea from home was probably not a luxury to be afforded men like Solomon, some serving long sentences here for as small a crime as stealing a loaf of bread.

If he and others did manage to escape, and few did, the closest they might come to a taste of the home country was a billy tea, twigs and all, brewed in an old tin can while the devils scampered through the high hedgerows planted by colonists lonely for familiar reminders of Mother Britain.

Tea of the British variety was not likely to have been given to the men who were originally transported to Van Diemen's Land. That was the original name given to the island by Dutch explorer Abel Tasman and it seemed appropriate for such a demonic place. No these men would to serve their time, then go on to populate and build the new country.

By comparison to what they could expect at afternoon teatime, my outdoor tea at Bonorong was as classy as tea at the Ritz. I think I may still have my tea towel with a damper recipe screened onto it and my tin cup with "Billy Tea" stamped on its side.

Beware Low-flying Tearooms
Signs of the speedy demise of Kiwi tearooms

A road sign in the little town of Mangaweka warned motorists to "Beware low-flying tearooms." It was a joke, of course, but it seemed to sum up New Zealand's attitude toward that most British of traditions, the taking of tea, at least the taking of it in fine quality tearooms.

Beware the 'proper' teashop with good linen, polished silver and the tinkle of fine china. Beware the tranquillity of good old-fashioned afternoon tea. Make way for the mighty Jo. Beware the nervous cries of the coffee-mad denizens of towns big and small across this tiny three-island country at the bottom of the earth.

Why the coffee squadrons have even strafed the tearoom that once existed in the gutted fuselage of the old Douglas DC-3 aircraft at Mangaweka. A postcard once referred to the "popular tearoom" there, but new literature had converted the famous landmark to a "café."

"Storm in a coffee cup" was the title of a painting on the cover of the Wellington phonebook that year. It might have read tempest in a teapot. The artist said she was inspired by the "city's ambience" and clearly that ambience smacked of coffee, not tea. Flipping through the *Wellington Yellow Pages*, I found a full page of listings for cafés, dozens of them. But there wasn't a single shop devoted to serving the whims and pleasures of tea drinkers.

Quite simply, New Zealand was bent on forsaking the brown leaf for the brown bean when I lived there in the late 1990s. In those days, Kiwis were making the conversion to java as fast as popular rugby players were sprinting to join the better-paying teams in the United Kingdom. Tearooms were reincarnated as cafés so hastily that the word 'tearoom' was simply stroked out and 'café' substituted on their signs.

When you found yourself thirsting for a cuppa in Kiwi towns like Mangaweka, you would instead opt for coffee. For on one side of the street would be an establishment called a tearoom. On the other, you would find a sophisticated café enticing you inside with a sporty hand-painted sign. It might say Medici's Café or Espresso Express or just plain The Coffee House.

Inside the tearoom you would find meat pies dying untold deaths under a heat lamp. Canned soup, white-sliced bread, greeting cards, soda pop and possibly some basic camping gear would be on sale in various corners. There would be an ice-cream freezer and a newspaper stand taking up space that might have been devoted to a collection of colourful tea caddies.

Inside the cafe, by contrast, you would be won over instantly by the exotic surroundings and equally exotic offerings. They would mesmerize you with enticing phrases like 'Come in and have a tasty cappuccino with cinnamon' or 'Sit down and enjoy a frothy latte with a fresh-baked cake' or 'Take a load off and have a mochaccino or a macchiato.'

Over in the darkest corners of the tearoom cum general store would be a lonely soul sitting at a Formica-topped table in a vinyl-covered kitchen chair. He or she would be sipping from a nondescript mug with a tea-bag string hanging out of it.

At the café, everyone would be drinking "short blacks" and "flat whites" out of big, round, stylish cups with saucers while relaxing in a fancy, padded, easy chair set on a cosy verandah. There might be fresh-cut flowers on the table, possibly a colourful tablecloth and maybe even cloth napkins. Which one would you choose?

Of course, there were exceptions, but only a few. John Muir, an Auckland tea importer of the day, explained why. "Tea is so 'at home' to Kiwis. You can get a cuppa at some of the hotels, but the fashionability of coffee has taken over. We're not tea philistines. We're as 'cup of tea' as any British national. Were buying about $200 million worth of tea a year, but tea tasters would be appalled at the quality."

He soon disabused me of any notion that this was a connoisseur tea-drinking country. New Zealanders were more likely to visit one of their thriving wineries than seek out the comfort of a tearoom. And perhaps that was understandable. From the early days, social class differences probably meant that quality tea drinking was restricted to the well-to-do Kiwi.

Working-class settlers had little time to dawdle at a quaint little tearoom for afternoon snacks and a cup of Assam or Darjeeling. Few would have had the money to start a teashop in any event. Those were rugged times requiring tough pioneer spirits. In fact, strong spirits may have been what filled any teacups that survived the three-month sea voyage without being shattered to pieces.

There is the odd tea crusader, of course. In the late 1990s, Anna Selak was among them. She wanted a place to sell her homemade teapots, so she founded Tea Total to sell the pots as much as to be a "purveyor of gourmet tea" in Auckland.

"Why has tea been left behind?" she asked in *Café* magazine. "Here in New Zealand we consume around two kilos of tea per person each year," she wrote. But Kiwis treat tea drinking "like morning ablutions, done but not discussed."

She had tried to lead by example in the battle against the coffee battalions, and her little teashop was a delight when I visited. Outside on the walk sat a few small round wooden tables with metal legs. Beside the door stood a wooden monkey holding a tray with a lovely hand-painted teapot on it.

"That's Peegee," she explained. "You know, for PG Tips." It was but one of many innovative ideas she had introduced. Peegee attracted the kids and the parents were soon sniffing curiously about the entrance. To lure them inside, Salek gave them something to do at her 'Sniffing Wall'. The old and young 'grungies' cohabited at the inside tables, listening to a slow blues tune waving invisibly through the air and lingering just long enough before changing to something classical.

Alas, Salek and a courageous few others were losing the war to ensure that cure-for-cancer tea could co-exist next to bad-for-your-health coffee. The struggle to get Kiwis to demand quality tearooms in the world's biggest Polynesian city, and in little towns like Mangaweka, was dying a speedy death.

As I was leaving New Zealand, Seattle-based Starbucks, the

mother of all trendy coffee chains (a.k.a. the McDonald's of the coffee world) was planning to flood into the neighbourhood. For the crusaders, the rallying cry might have been 'Tea drinkers unite. You have nothing to lose but your bags' or 'Give tea chance.' But I feared that neither cry would be heard or heeded.

Postscript
Tea on the outer edge of Antarctica

If you want to eat muttonbird in the last English-speaking town before you reach Antarctica, you go to the South Sea Hotel restaurant at the very bottom of New Zealand on Stewart Island, the country's almost forgotten "third island." If it's tea you want, go to JustCafé.

That was the advice I got at the Invercargill airport when I was waiting for the weather to change over Foveaux Strait so that my small plane could take off and land safely on the other side. It was close to the end of a long draught in those parts but the airport ticket man said the plane wouldn't land unless we could see the tops of the surrounding trees.

Eventually the rain stopped, the treetops peeked through the mist, the plane landed, and then took off for Oban, the tiny capital of Stewart Island.

JustCafé has rightly put the other local 'tearooms' to shame with its upbeat city fare. All the Obanians recommended a stop at the nicely appointed shop with its wooden chairs and tables, backgammon board and attractive dried lavender bouquets hanging from the ceiling.

It's a trendy place that doesn't pay much attention to what's considered the latest fad on the mainland. Owner Britt Moore had a Starbucks twenty-fifth birthday poser mounted in the side dining area. But she doesn't serve that trendy fast-coffee-and-tea brand.

Britt had the usual selection of teas and coffees, but she advertised them with flair. One can order a "Foveaux Espresso" for $2.50, a "Totally Wired" double espresso for $3 or a "Cappo" with Attitude (cappuccino with marshmallows and chocolate flake) for $4.50.

Non-coffee drinkers can opt for a big bowl of "Save the Whales," chocolate, marshmallow and a chocolate fish. Then there's her *pièce de résistance* for tea drinkers: the "Teapuccino." To make it, Britt put some loose tea through the cappuccino machine to foam it up.

"I'm a resource manager," Britt said who is originally from Iowa. "I did my PhD in social geography and my case study was on Stewart Island." She specialised in the public consultation process in tourism development. Her conclusion: there wasn't much for it.

Britt stayed on the island for six years. She started her cafe cum tearoom in 1997 and at the time was operating it five months a year. For the other seven months, residents of this quirky little island must do without her savoury muffins, tasty quiches and home-made broccoli and cheese soup.

A resourceful manager, indeed, Britt makes all the food herself. For example, for her salmon sandwiches she uses locally caught salmon smoked in Dunedin, New Zealand's Scottish city. Some local also goes into her scrumptious apple-cheese torte, blueberry muffins and brownies.

She regularly consults a local cookbook, too. *Tried and True Recipes* by Marion Whipp includes everything from "sherried sausages" to Steward Island pavlova.

It isn't your typical tearoom but given the paucity of quality tearooms in New Zealand, JustCafé offers quite a memorable tea experience out on the lower edge of the world at Halfmoon Bay. And the "teapuccino" isn't as bad as it might sound to tea lovers.

8 CONCLUSION

"[I am] a hardened and shameless tea drinker, who has for many years diluted his meals with only the infusion of this fascinating plant; whose kettle scarcely has time to cool; who with tea amuses the evening, with tea solaces the midnight, and with tea welcomes the morning."

– From a letter written by Dr. Samuel Johnson in 1757.

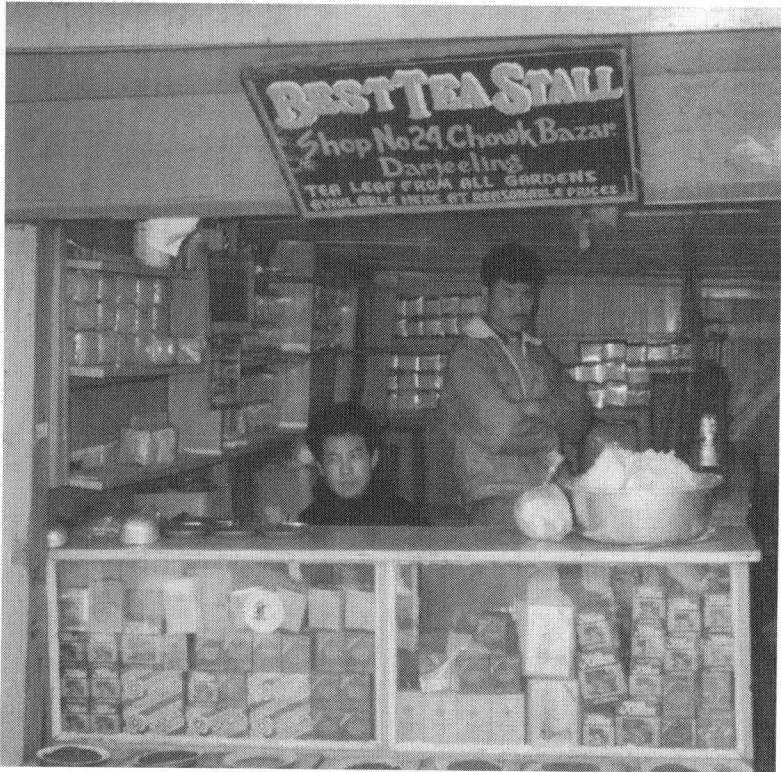

Tea merchants displaying their product at the Chowk
Bazaar in Darjeeling, India.

Tea Lands Yet to Conquer
And now back to that quiet tea time of the wanderer's soul

So ends my personal tour through some of the world's great tearooms and a few that were not so great. As you have read, I seldom missed an opportunity to visit a far-off tea oasis. The prospect of a new tea experience seldom failed to lure me even when I knew that the reality would not always live up to the previously advertised promise. Success or failure, the process of getting there was never fruitless.

Tea Leaves, then, is meant to be read as a travel memoir more than a traveller's guide to the tea places I have visited in various exotic parts of the world. Indeed, I owe readers an apology if they discover that some of my favourite tearooms have disappeared with the onslaught of coffee that is sweeping the world of the New Millenium.

Tearooms were seldom the primary reason for my travelling to distant lands, but somehow they began to serve as a kind of North Star, a compass point to steer towards as I visited the tea lands on quite a different mission. Thus they evolved into my refuge from the nerve-wracking details of travel and work, offering places to rest, write, read and soak up an ambience created by the long and rich history of tea.

I started my tea leaves many years ago, little knowing the breadth and depth of the world I was invading. By now you are no doubt tea-logged with my stories of that invasion. For friends and colleagues, it might have seemed an odd choice for a person like me. After all, I was not of the tea world.

Mine was a far more frantic and harsh political world wherein tea was scoffed at as a pastime of the rich and powerful. Royalty took tea; commoners slurped it down at workplace tea sheds. Wealthy corporate executives' wives sipped tea from priceless china tea cups and delicately dangled a little finger as they took bites of crustless watercress and cucumber sandwiches.

So it must have been strange to some of my colleagues and friends watching me indulge in such a seemingly bourgeois pastime. Was this working-class stiff selling out to high society? Why wasn't he studying pub life instead of tea life? Surely that was closer to his roots and far more interesting.

On my return to work after one long journey to the tea lands, my boss walked through my office door with a smirk on his face. He had discovered a publisher's proof of one of my *Tea Leaves* articles in the fax machine and exclaimed how out of character it was for me to be writing about something as innocuous and irrelevant as tea.

Perhaps he was right. Perhaps I should have been penning yet another pamphlet about the evils of an inherently unfair system, slamming corporate greed or damning another sell-out politician. But to escape all of that for a few moments each day, to find peace and tranquillity away from the din, this is what tearooms represented to me. Despite what seemed to me to be denigrating looks, I wasn't prepared to relinquish my taste for tea travel.

Soon the oldest hot drink in the world began to hold historical interest for me. It had long been a working-class drink as much as that of any other class. When working people finally were able to afford it, they poured it down by the boatload. It replaced beer and other spirits and that was a social change of great positive consequence. The world of commerce and international trade once flourished around tea. Transportation technology was changed by fast tea clippers like the famed Cutty Sark that sped from China and India back to Europe with their precious leaf cargo.

My tea leaves allowed me to enter a far-flung world of history, adventure, even mystery. They taught me that whatever a person chooses to do, it is possible to discover there a wealth of meaningful educational experiences. Along the way, I was treated to the delicacies of the finest tea tables in existence.

I didn't realize, for example, that whole countries could be classified as tea-drinking nations while others could be dubbed coffee countries. Nor did I realize the full historical significance of tea. I knew about the Boston Tea Party, of course, but not very much about it. I had heard of the drive to bring the brown leaf to the markets of Europe from Asia. I had read about the tea connection to the Opium Wars of the nineteenth century. I knew of the travels of Marco Polo to tea lands never before visited from the West. I had visited the Cutty Sark tea clipper in London, the teapot museum in Norwich, East Anglia, and the great tea estates of Darjeeling where tea workers harvested the green gold that would go on sale in the major markets of Europe, North America and around the world.

I had not realized how many people earn their living from tea or how many countries' economies swing back and forth on the fortunes of tea exports. In this age of Starbucks and various coffee copycats offering tea as an afterthought, it might be hard to imagine whole nations holding to a tea-drinking tradition. Astonishing as it may seem to some, much of the world continues to drink tea and has done so for about 4,000 years.

Tea is so much a part of some cultures, so important in Japan, for example, that complex ceremonies have been associated with it for centuries. In others, it is such a routine part of the local economy, such as in Turkey, for example, as to be almost invisible. It has a matter-of-fact omnipresence there and in many other countries that continue to embrace tea.

I have touched here on some of the history of tea and tearooms, but my intent was not to make you an expert in tea lore. Rather, it was to take you with me on a tea-lover's tour where you could relax and enjoy the ride, letting me be your guide.

Did I treat you to a taste of yak butter tea with Buddhist monks in the peaks of Tibet? No. Did we have Russian caravan tea served from a samovar before a visit to the Hermitage in St. Petersburg? No. Did we get to Kyoto to have a geisha pamper us with whisked tea during a Japanese tea ceremony? No. Did we sip Africa tea while on safari in Kenya or floating past the great pyramids near Cairo? No.

Did we drink yerba maté through a metal-tipped straw from a gourd with Aboriginal people in South America? No. Did we make tea over an open fire after breaking into a hard tea brick freed from a saddle bag while riding horseback along the Silk Road? No. Did we experience the ultimate luxury of taking high tea on the Orient Express? No.

I failed you on all these counts. I also failed to reach the great tearooms of Europe in sufficient number. For example, I did not visit a single tearoom in the Netherlands where tea was first imported from the Far East to be stored under lock and key in the tea caddies of European aristocracy.

Nor was I fortunate enough to explore the tearooms of Germany in Hanover, Hamburg, Bonn and Berlin. And what of tea in Scandinavia? Surely I have missed many an opportunity to take you with me on tea leaves to Copenhagen, Oslo and Stockholm.

In fact, there are many tea leaves still on my planning table. Many tea lands yet to visit. There are the tea estates in Assam, heading towards Bangla Desh, or those around Nilgiri in southern Indian or around Kandi, Sri Lanka, or the Cameron Highlands of Malaysia to name a few.

But from the tea leaves I did manage to take, I drew the following rather subjective philosophical conclusions: Tea is calm, coffee frantic. Tea is safe, coffee dangerous. Tea is peace, coffee war. Tea is history, coffee modern. Tea is truth, coffee gossip. Tea is literature, coffee journalism. Tea is rural, coffee urban. Tea is healthy, coffee is not. Tea is the waltz; coffee is the mambo, the watusi, the cha, cha, cha. Tea is the Beatles, coffee the Rolling Stones. Tea cures cancer, coffee enhances your chances of getting it. Tea is life, coffee is ulcers. Tea is heaven, coffee can lead to hell.

I hope I have succeeded in treating you to something special and that I have whet your appetite to take some tea leaves of your own. If I have provided a momentary escape from the fast-paced, market-mad new world that is increasingly coffee-driven, then my mission is accomplished.

We live in an age of war and terror. The four horsemen of the apocalypse gallop through the world as if they had coffee hot-wired into their veins. The tea time of the soul seems lost for the moment. Perhaps the answer is to return to a quieter more peaceful time when the world stopped each day for an hour or so, when people put aside everything else to enjoy a brief respite with their favourite cuppa.

I leave you now to contemplate those bygone times and to map out future tea leaves in hopes that the world can find a way to join me.

Ron Verzuh

ABOUT THE AUTHOR

Ron Verzuh is a writer, photographer and historian who has travelled the world for more than thirty years in search of the perfect cup of tea in the perfect tearoom. His articles on tea have appeared in newspapers, magazines, newsletters and web sites in Canada, New Zealand and the United Kingdom. He obtained his undergraduate degree in English literature from Simon Fraser University in 1972, his Master's degree in Canadian studies from Carleton University in 1985 and is completing his PhD in history at Simon Fraser University. He has been a regular columnist for *content*, Canada's media magazine, and *Canadian Consumer*, published by the Consumer's Association of Canada. He is the author of several essays, monographs and many articles on subjects ranging from social movements and politics to travel, literature, news media, film, food, consumerism and health. Much of his work can be seen at his web site: www.ronverzuh.ca. Ron Verzuh currently lives in Eugene, Oregon.

The author enjoying tea with Mithra the ape
at the Singapore Zoo.

YOUR TEA TRAVELLING
NOTES AND INTINERARIES

Made in the USA
Lexington, KY
25 May 2012